Teens, Technology, and Literacy

TEENS, TECHNOLOGY, AND LITERACY

Or, Why Bad Grammar Isn't Always Bad

Linda W. Braun

Foreword by Pam Berger

LIBRARIES

UNLIMITED

A Member of the Greenwood Publishing Group

Westport, Connecticut • London

Library of Congress Cataloging-in-Publication Data

Braun, Linda W.
   Teens, technology, and literacy, or, Why bad grammar isn't always bad / Linda W. Braun; foreword by Pam Berger.
      p. cm.
   Includes bibliographical references and index.
   ISBN 1-59158-368-3 (alk. paper)
     1. Computers and literacy—United States.   2. Literacy—Social aspects—United States.   3. Technological literacy—United States.   4. Technology and youth—United States.   5. Teenagers—Social networks—United States.   I. Title.   II. Title: Why bad grammar isn't always bad.
   LC149.5.B73 2007
   373.133'4—dc22   2006031714

British Library Cataloguing in Publication Data is available.

Library of Congress Catalog Card Number: 2006031714
ISBN: 1-59158-368-3

First published in 2007

Libraries Unlimited, 88 Post Road West, Westport, CT 06881
A Member of the Greenwood Publishing Group, Inc.
www.lu.com

Printed in the United States of America

The paper used in this book complies with the
Permanent Paper Standard issued by the National
Information Standards Organization (Z39.48–1984).

10 9 8 7 6 5 4 3 2 1

Once more for Robert and Lucy,
who kept their humor as I wrote,
obsessed, and asked for advice

Contents

List of Figures   xi
Foreword   xiii
Introduction   xv

I. DEFINING LITERACY   1

1   What Is Literacy Really? 3
A Simple Definition   3
A Brief History of Literacy   5
    Literacy as a Skill   6
    Literacy as School Knowledge   6
    Literacy as a Social and School Construct   7
Where Are We Now?   8
    More Aspects of Literacy   8
    Literacy and Identity   9

II. LITERACY IN TECHNOLOGY ENVIRONMENTS   11

2   The World of Messaging 13
The How and Why of Language Conventions in
   Real-Time Virtual Environments   14
    IM   14
    Text Messaging   17
Supporting IM and Texting Literacies in Libraries and Classrooms   19

IM Literacies in the Library and Classroom 19
Texting Literacies in the Library and Classroom 22
Advancement, Not Decline 23

3 Out There for the World: Blogs, Wikis, Podcasts 25
Teen Bloggers 27
Public Blogging 27
Blogger Identity 30
Saying Something Meaningful 31
Reading in a Blogger's World 33
Reading the Audience 33
Blog Integration 34
Wikis 35
Wiki Pros and Cons 36
Writing History 37
Beyond Wikipedia 37
Teens and Wikis 37
Wiki Literacies 39
Hear All About It—Podcasting 39
Podcasting and Identity 40
Worldwide Listenership 41
The Listening Experience 42
The Creating Experience 43
Listener Attention 43
Musical Life 44
Putting the Pieces Together 45

4 Making Connections with Tagging. 47
A Keyword by Any Other Name 47
Beyond the Blog 49
Out of the Chaos 52
Information Literacy Can't Be Ignored 53
Comparing Technologies 54
Making Meaning 55
Considering Tag Clouds 55
When, Where, Why 56

5 Reading and Writing in a Gamer's World. 57
It's All There 58
Good Learning from Good Games 59
Making the Sell 62
No Game Play is Entirely Passive 62

Gamers Do Not Play (or Live) in a Vacuum 63
The Gamer's World is Not an Entirely Evil World 63
Focus on Literacy 63
Workshop Gaming 65
Go Beyond Availability 65
Fad or Not 66

III. LIBRARIES AND CLASSROOMS AS VIRTUAL COMMUNITIES 69

6 Technology + Literacy = Social Networking 71
Defining Community 71
MySpace 73
The Library and School Build Teen Social Networks .. 74
My Own Café 75
Friendster 76
Hennepin County Library Catalog 77
The Perfect Library or Classroom Social Network 78
Building Social Networks at Your Library or in Your Classroom 79
Talking Points 79
No Dust 82

7 A World of Ideas 83
Integrating Instant and Text Messaging—Round-Up, Chapter 2 83
Integrating Blogs, Wikis, and Podcasts—Round-Up, Chapter 3 84
Integrating Tagging—Round-Up, Chapter 4 86
Integrating Gaming—Round-Up, Chapter 5 87
Social Networking—Round-Up, Chapter 6 88
Making it Work 89

Appendix A—Web-Based Content Creation Tools 91

Appendix B—Finding and Catching Blogs and Podcasts .. 93

Appendix C—All About Technology 97

References 99

Index 103

List of Figures

2.1 Pew Internet & American Life Project: Parents
& Teens 2004 Survey 16

3.1 Sunday Morning Blog 28

3.2 Sample Wikipedia History Screen 38

4.1 Sunday Morning Blogger Interests 48

4.2 43 Things Tag Cloud 51

4.3 Apple/MAC Tag Cloud 56

6.1 Levels of Teen Communities 72

6.2 My Own Café 75

Foreword

Pam Berger

Did you respond to the blog posting? Have you listened to the latest podcast? Did you contribute to the class wiki? These are not questions from a current science fiction novel but rather student interactions in twenty-first-century classrooms and libraries. What it means to be literate is changing. Web 2.0, the term coined for the next generation Web, moves the Internet from being simply Web sites and search engines to a shared network space that offers students a place to publish and broadcast their own writing, collaborate on projects, and engage in conversations. Students with their mobile and nonmobile devices—cell phones, MP3 players, laptops, digital cameras, computers— are always online and connected to one another and to the Web. The first traces of Web 2.0 are appearing in the form of classroom blogs and wikis and Web sites such as Flickr, My Space, and LibraryThing—displaying the Web 2.0 principles of interactivity, user participation, and collective intelligence.

We know learning needs to be authentic to be relevant to our students. It's critical that when teaching literacy to our students we emphasize skills that reflect the information environment of the present, not the past. These new tools—Weblogs, wikis, podcasts, RSS, and IM—enable everyday Internet users to disseminate their ideas and experience and communicate in a seamless 24/7 environment. They are challenging educators to reevaluate their definition of literacy. What does it mean to be literate in this environment? How can these new tools support literacy? How do I use these tools in the curriculum?

For those of us who have worked with issues of technology integration for last few decades, it has always been about teaching literacy, curriculum, and content understandings, not using technology for its own sake but to support teaching and learning to create independent thinkers and lifelong learners. Accordingly, the strategies introduced in this book empower classroom teachers and librarians to develop authentic, relevant learning experiences that will prepare students to be literate in the twenty-first century.

In this text Linda Braun invites us, as learner-educators, to cross the threshold and enter the world of teen literacy in the twenty-first century. Here we get a glimpse into complex, technologically rich environments where teens write, read, collaborate, publish, and communicate; an environment where students text message to check on their homework, IM about favorite books with the librarian, keep online journals reacting to the world and their research efforts via blogs, use wikis to keep group notes and information about their research topic, listen to podcasts created by fellow students and teachers, and interact in games and social spaces provided by their library. We are challenged by the author to poke and prod at these technologies not only to understand the literacy implications, but also their importance to teens—intellectually, emotionally, and socially.

As Mark Prensky points out, today's students are native speakers of technology, fluent in the digital language of computers and the Internet, whereas most adults (teachers and librarians) are digital immigrants who were not born into the digital world. We have adopted many aspect of technology, but just like those who learn another language later in life, we retain an "accent" because we still have one foot in the past (Prensky 2001). As educators, we need to understand how teens use these tools to communicate, and exploit the power of these technologies to support teaching and learning and, most important, literacy. As educators, we know well that learning takes doing. Linda provides a chapter summarizing the technology integration ideas mentioned in the text to encourage readers to get actively involved, and select a few to try immediately.

This book is for educators who want to understand the digital native's world and how it has changed and enhanced teen literacy. It challenges teachers and librarians to think differently about technology's potential to support literacy.

Introduction

Making Sense to a Larger Audience

This is a book I've wanted to write for a very long time.

Over the past several years friends and family listened to me talk about the positive implications technology has for teen reading and writing skills. In many of these conversations I felt like people didn't understand the issues the way I understood them. Others didn't seem to see the same landscape I saw. I sometimes even felt like I was living on another planet.

In the past two years, however, several technologies have risen to the forefront in the press, in education, and in day-to-day conversation. Others have spoken out and written books and articles on the types of topics that I've been trying to promote. Librarians and educators are noting the work of Steven Johnson, the author of *Everything Bad Is Good for You*, and James Gee, the author of *What Video Games Have to Teach Us About Literacy and Learning*. Each of these authors discusses how technology and popular culture have an impact on learning and life. Their writing resonates with readers.

As a result of this more open dialogue there is a new readiness for the conversations I have tried to initiate. The technologies (of which some are new and some have been around for quite a while) discussed by Johnson, Gee, and others are the technologies teens use every day to communicate with each other, family, and teachers. They are the technologies that give teens the chance to collaborate and create. They are:

- Technologies that require that teens go beyond passive use to active involvement in planning, creating, and editing
- Technologies such as IM, chat, Weblogs, wikis, and podcasts
- Technologies that are no longer tools for and of the future, but of the present day that expand and enhance learning and thinking and have become part of a way of life

Each of the technologies has significant implications for teen reading and writing skills. The conversation that I have longed for, and that can now take place with more open ears, is one that explores how these tools are not inherently evil, but actually, in many instances, how they create stronger rather than weaker teen literacy skills.

Early in *Everything Bad Is Good For You* Steven Johnson writes, "The sky is not falling. In many ways the weather has never been better. It just takes a new kind of barometer to tell the difference." (Johnson 2005, xiv) My goal with this book is to help educators learn how to read the new kind of barometer that Johnson mentions and see that the positive literacy implications and possibilities for technology loom large. And while there are also some possible negative implications, we cannot allow those to deter us from harnessing the good in order to support teens' interests, educational needs, and search for identity.

As a matter of fact, librarians and teachers must not fear what technology brings or decide that in order to protect teens it's better to keep them away from the new tools and what they can do with them. Librarians and teachers must work to understand why teens use these tools and help their colleagues, parents, peers, and administrators understand that the technology tools teens embrace are a vital and important part of teen life. Taking these tools away, saying "you can't use them because they might lead to dangerous situations," doesn't do teens, librarians, or society any good. It only creates an atmosphere of us vs. them, and an atmosphere in which teens are forced to try to get away with something.

I believe that by focusing on specific technologies, teachers, librarians, and parents will gain new ideas and inspiration that will help them support teens' educational and recreational needs. It will also give adults who live and work with teens an ability to articulate the positive aspects of teen technology use.

Perhaps after reading this book a teacher will decide to integrate online interactive technologies in her classroom. Or maybe a librarian will decide to experiment with building online communities with the teens with whom she works. Perhaps both teachers and librarians will begin to realize that what teens are trying out with technology isn't bad because it's different. They will understand that it's just different, and that's not necessarily bad.

WHAT'S NOT INSIDE

This book is not a how-to on setting up a blog, running a podcast, or setting up a wiki. (In reading the pages it is, however, possible to learn what the technologies discussed are, and understand the opportunities they provide schools and libraries.) Instead, it is an exploration of the implications of technology on teen reading, writing, and learning skills and habits. This book also provides the conceptual framework and language needed in order to help make a case to colleagues, administrators, parents, and community members about the key role that new and emerging technologies play in a teen's literacy growth.

WHAT IS INSIDE

This volume is divided into three parts.

PART I: DEFINING LITERACY

The first section sets up a framework for the definition of literacy that is used throughout this book. The chapter briefly looks at literacy within a historical context and then describes what the idea of literacy means for teens in the early twenty-first century. This literacy overview helps guarantee that readers of this book understand the perspective presented in the chapters that follow the first section.

PART II: LITERACY IN TECHNOLOGY ENVIRONMENTS

The chapters in the second part of the book look at a variety of technology tools that teens currently use and explain what the tools are and how they support teen literacy needs. The technologies include those that teens use on a regular basis to create content as well as those they use to communicate with peers, family, and teachers or librarians. Along with information on the literacy aspects of a variety of tools, these chapters also contain information about how the tools can be used in classrooms and libraries to help enhance teen literacy practices and skills.

PART III: LIBRARIES AND CLASSROOMS AS VIRTUAL COMMUNITIES

There is no doubt that the library of the twenty-first century must change in order to meet the needs of customers—no matter what the age. Part of this change is in presenting programs and services to teenagers that enable them to use the tools and technology they require for learning and for leisure. The library described in this section of the book is a library in which teens are a part of a virtual community that librarians (with teens) help organize and deliver. Within this virtual community teens use the technology tools with which they are familiar to learn, collaborate, create, and communicate. In this community the library is central to the teen's ability to succeed.

WELCOME THE POSSIBILITIES

As mentioned above, it has taken almost a decade for the world to accept the gains to literacy as a result of technology use by teens. Of course, during that decade, people continued to write and discuss the positives, but really listening to and understanding the ideas was limited. Librarians and educators no longer have the leisure to wait many years in order to accept something that their customers—teens—want to use, and are using, whether the librarians and educators accept that use or not. In addition to providing information and insights to readers, it is my hope that this book will provide a jumping-off point for further research and investigation into the ways teens use technology to enhance literacy. Once you have finished reading the ideas contained in this book, welcome the technology and literacy possibilities. Go out and:

- Talk to teens about the way they use technology to read or write—either for leisure or education
- Give up assumptions
- Read teen blogs on a regular basis
- Subscribe to and listen to teen podcasts
- Set up a wiki
- Use text messaging
- Use IM
- Keep up with what's happening in the world of teen technology use

- Build your own online social network
- And again, give up assumptions

It really is all about assumptions. For too long librarians and educators have assumed that technology does more harm than good when it comes to teen literacy skills and practices. Now, people are finally realizing that this is not the case. Instead of assuming the negative or the worst, the next time a new technology used by teens is mentioned, investigate it by trying it out. (Don't assume you know what it does and how it's used simply by reading and hearing about it.) Then force yourself to consider the positive aspects of the technology on teen literacy. I hope this book will be a starting place for knowing just how to do that.

PART I

Defining Literacy

The meanings of literacy in a historic and educational context and an overview of how literacy is defined within the pages of this book

1

What is Literacy Really?

> How you define literacy often depends upon your own personal perspectives. Much of the current confusion results from the word being used in a daunting variety of contexts, such as computer literacy, cultural literacy, numerical literacy, reading literacy, art literacy, and financial literacy. (Gordon and Gordon 2003, 16)

Literacy is a word used quite a bit by librarians, educators, and the general public. But what does it really mean? When thinking about the term it is reasonable to wonder:

- What exactly is literacy?
- Does everyone mean the same thing when using the word literacy?
- Do people define literacy the same way today as they did a decade ago?
- Do teachers, librarians, and the general public define literacy in the same way?
- Is literacy the same as reading and writing skills?

A SIMPLE DEFINITION

These are questions that need to be addressed when considering how technology supports teen literacy. A place to start in gaining an understanding of what the term literacy means is, of course, the dictionary. The *American Heritage Dictionary* defines literacy this way: "The condition or quality of being literate, especially the ability to read and write" (American Heritage 1993, 762).

If you move on to look up the term literate, since that's a part of the definition of literacy, you'll find the primary definition is "Able to read and write" (American Heritage 1993, 762). It's therefore reasonable to assume that many people think of literacy as the ability to read and to write. That definition of course still leads to some very big questions. For example, the ability to read and write what? If a teenager is able to read emoticons used in chat rooms successfully can that teenager be considered literate? If a teenager is able to read and write blogs but has trouble with Shakespeare, can we consider that teen literate?

This is where we tend to get into murky territory when it comes to technology and its impact on teen literacy. Adults working with teens often believe that the text literacies teens exhibit when working with technology don't "count" as much as the literacies teens exhibit when reading and writing in traditional print formats. To use a cliché, if I had a nickel for every time a librarian, teacher, or other adult lamented the fact that teens weren't reading and writing because of all the time they spent online in chat rooms, My Space, blogs, and so on I'd be a wealthy woman. But in reality, every time a teenager is using one of those technological tools she is exhibiting literacy skills.

"… most studies of reading ignore the huge explosion in reading (not to mention writing) that has happened thanks to the rise of the Internet. Millions of people spend most of their day staring at words on a screen: browsing the Web, reading email, chatting with friends, posting a new entry in one of those 8 million blogs … you're putting words together yourself, and not just digesting someone else's. Part of the compensation for reading less is the fact that we are writing more." (Johnson 2005, 183)

What if you kept a log of every time you read something or wrote something during a 24-hour period? What would be in that log? For many people it would include reading the newspaper, reading a magazine article or book, writing an e-mail, or writing a report or memo. There are multiple reading and writing opportunities that you experience every day. Some are probably technology-based and some are probably more traditionally print-based. However, every time you read or write during that 24-hour period you are exhibiting at least some form and level of literacy.

What if you asked the teenagers with whom you work or live to keep track of every time they read or write during a 24-hour period? What would be in their log? Perhaps the log would include a notation about music videos, because those videos always include text with the name of the song or artist. Perhaps IM interchanges with friends would be included, because every time a teen sends or receives an IM they are reading or writing. Perhaps text messages sent during the day would be included, because one can't message without reading and writing. The list might even include downloading music from iTunes. To accomplish that download a teen has to read the name of the artist and song and follow download directions and might even have to enter text into a screen in order to make the purchase.

Most likely the teen's log of his or her literacy experiences during a one-day period would be extremely full. The teen might even include more literacy experiences than you would. The teen's activities might be both similar and different from your own. If there are differences, does it mean that your literacy activities are better than the teen's? Are you more literate because of the types of literacy activities with which you are involved? Not necessarily. Steven Johnson, as mentioned in the introduction, suggests that we need to use a different barometer in order to gauge the changes technology brings to the world. Determining what constitutes literate practices in the early twenty-first century definitely requires a new barometric device. Being different doesn't mean not being literate. It just means expanding the concept of what is means to be literate.

A BRIEF HISTORY OF LITERACY

In order to gain more perspective on what constitutes literacy let's look at the ways in which definitions of literacy within an educational context have changed, and the ways in which they have remained the same, over time. In an article on the history of literacy Arlette Willis breaks down the definition of literacy into three categories as a way to demonstrate how the meaning of the term has changed over time and how distinctive groups have defined literacy differently—historians vs. educators for example. The categories Willis lays out are:

- literacy as a skill
- literacy as school knowledge
- literacy as social and school construct (Willis 1997)

The following section of this chapter uses Willis' categories as a means of looking at how literacy was, and is, defined. By doing this, a foundation for the meaning of literacy—as used within the pages of this book—is laid out.

Literacy as a Skill

This definition of literacy is one that focuses simply on the ability of anyone to read and write. (This corresponds to the dictionary definition stated above.) Defining it as only related to these skills, however, makes literacy seem much more simplistic than it really is. In order to connect reading skill to writing skill the reader has to be able to deconstruct the text and determine what the writer does well, or not so well. The literacy of reading and writing is therefore more than knowing how to pronounce the words and understand their meaning.

Willis notes in her article that historically this definition has had social, economic, cultural, and political links. For example, the simple ability to read and write is connected to the learner's ability to acquire the education needed to gain the skill. The better the education, the more likely it is that the learner not only has the skills but also has a high level of skill. These connections also point to the fact that the skill of literacy may be defined differently over time, so that what was once considered skillful within one social or political framework may be defined differently at another point in time.

When thinking about literacy in the early twenty-first century, it is clear that these links relate specifically to skills that were nonexistent in previous decades and that teens demonstrate today as a form of literacy. Being able to write coherently within the various technological formats available to them is a skill that is important today and that demonstrates reading and writing literacy in the technological age.

The danger in defining literacy within the skill framework only is that it doesn't fully take into account skill levels within the context of societal needs and expectations. This seemingly simple method of defining literacy has a direct connection to the next category in Willis' framework—literacy as school knowledge.

Literacy as School Knowledge

Historically, when looking at literacy as school knowledge, the focus is on something that is simply related to cognition and that can be tested within a school environment. Willis writes, "In summary, definitions and purposes of literacy-as-school-knowledge suggest that literacy is a cognitive skill that can be measured and interpreted as an indicator of intelligence and school achievement." (Willis 1997, 391) An implication of this is that the world in which the learner lives—home, school, playground, and arcade—does not have any relevance to how literate he is; literacy is only learned and exhibited within the classroom and on school grounds.

This is the definition that in the past was frequently used when assessing reading and writing literacy through standardized tests. As a result, these tests often did not take into account outside forces that play a role in a test-taker's literacy skills. Willis notes that in more recent years this definition has grown to encompass societal connections to literacy (the impact a teenager's home life has on his or her literacy, for example). Yet, programs like No Child Left Behind focus strongly on the definition of literacy as school knowledge.

Think about how limited this definition is within a technology context. Teens are constantly reading and writing outside of the school environment. They send text messages from the mall. They blog from home. They read RSS feeds at the public library. (See chapter 3 for a definition of RSS.) If the only measure of teens' literacy skills is how successfully they read and write in the classroom—on assignments, tests, and so on—then those assessing the skills miss a huge and integral part of teens' reading and writing life. Teen reading and writing might even be stronger and more frequent in nonschool situations than in school situations. Shouldn't those count within the literacy skill assessment arena?

Literacy as a Social and School Construct

This definition of literacy—which became popular in the late twentieth century—focuses on recognizing that literacy practices and skills vary based on economic, social, political, and cultural associations. Within this definition, where one lives, who is in one's family, what one does in his or her spare time, what school is like for a specific learner, and so on have direct implications for literacy practices and skills.

This definition recognizes that in order for reading and writing to be meaningful they have to be connected to the reader's/writer's real world. It also acknowledges that a reader's/writer's personal identity is wrapped up in their literacy practices. What teens read and what they write help them determine who they are. This is largely the definition of literacy used in this book.

The reason the tie is so strong is because it provides opportunities to discuss and acknowledge how teens use technology to communicate with others and express their thoughts and feelings. It leaves open the possibility of recognizing that when a teen writes a text message to a friend she is using a literacy skill. It allows for integrating the use of personal blog space as an example of positive literacy applications. It guarantees that teens who read and write comfortably and for pleasure outside of school should be considered literate in today's society.

WHERE ARE WE NOW?

While the definitions of literacy briefly described above go in and out of fashion over time, no one definition is completely accurate or completely inaccurate. As librarians and educators, we need to determine which kernels within each definition are correct and then meld those kernels together. This will help us design a definition that works for the twenty-first century and for the teens with whom we work.

Stop and consider what it means, within a global context, that definitions of literacy change over time. If the definition of literacy is not static (or stagnant) doesn't that mean that as technology is more and more a part of a teenager's demonstration of literacy an entirely new definition must emerge? If so, shouldn't that new definition take into account the contemporary ways that people read and write using the tools currently available? Or are the definitions based on skill, test results, and social environment broad enough that the new ways of reading and writing can be encompassed within those definitions? Willis includes two statements in her article that address these questions directly:

> As we find ourselves, at the end of the twentieth century, reflecting on our past accomplishments and setting priorities and goals for the twenty-first century, how we define literacy and the purposes we set for literacy are more important than ever.... (Willis 1997, 392)

> The reactions to past literacy crises have attempted to offer quick fix responses to literacy. I think we are living in the best of times to dismantle and deconstruct definitions and purposes for literacy that have created barriers to literacy in the past. The good old days for reconceptualizing how literacy is defined, for what purposes it is taught, and to whom, are now. (Willis 1997, 395)

More Aspects of Literacy

Let's look at a few more research perspectives on the topic of adolescent literacy. To start, consider the adolescent literacy position statement that was published by the International Reading Association in 2000. That statement sets out a series of principles and guidelines that support adolescent literacy development. One guideline that stands out within the context of this discussion states, "Adolescents deserve teachers who understand the complexities of individual adolescent readers, respect their differences, and respond to their characteristics" (Moore et al. 2000, 8).

This statement makes it clear that teenagers need opportunities to gain and improve literacy skills that allow for individual needs and interests. This includes interests that go beyond traditional literacy teaching techniques (for example, classic texts and textbooks) and require the inclusion of technology-based tools that promote text-based literacy. As Bronwyn Williams wrote, "If literacy is more than just decoding marks on a page, if it is shaped by culture and context, then the cultures and contexts we inhabit in our lives outside the classroom will necessarily influence the way we approach literacy practices in school" (Williams 2005/2006, 343). These cultures and contexts include online communications and recreational tools.

Literacy and Identity

Another aspect of this guideline not to ignore is the importance of teen identity. While the guideline doesn't specifically mention identity, the idea that teachers need to respect the unique interests and needs of each adolescent has a direct connection to recognizing that each teen has a specific identity and that that identity should be considered as a part of literacy practices.

As discussed in the following chapters, the opportunities technology provides to support and assist teens in their search for identity via reading and writing are profound. As teens read, they consider the people and events in that text and think about whether or not they might take on some or all of the traits of one or more characters represented. Research performed by a variety of educators demonstrates that adolescents use what they read as touchstones to the person they might become. Therefore, as teens read, they reconfigure their identities based on their reading (Thompson 2004, 48–49). Throughout this volume, consideration is placed on how the new technologies teens use engage them in literacy, and as a result support their need to develop an identity.

Literacy, no matter its form—print, information, visual, and so on— is more than understanding the words on the paper, the meaning of the image, or the best way to locate a piece of information. In order to be literate, a teen in the early twenty-first century must be able to perform the basic tasks of literacy and use those tasks as a way to make meaning about life and about the world in which they live.

In this book the definition of literacy takes into account a teen's search for identity and the school and social conditions in which a teen is immersed. The following chapters look at how text-based literacy is supported by technology and focuses on the idea that the teens who use nontraditional forms of reading and writing, the teens who communicate using new technologies, and the teens who develop new forms and formats of reading and writing demonstrate valid literacy practices and skills.

PART II

Literacy in Technology Environments

An exploration of the literacy implications of a variety of technologies with a look at how classrooms and libraries can integrate the technologies into their programs in order to support teen literacies

2

The World of Messaging

> Most linguists believe that after 10,000 years no traces of a language remain in its descendants.... Languages are perpetuated by the children who learn them. When linguists see a language spoken only by adults they know it is doomed. (Pinker 2000, 262)

Over and over again teachers and librarians lament the language teens use in real-time electronic communications. There is concern that using these technologies to communicate and using language that is not what one would traditionally consider grammatically correct will cause language and the future use of language to change, for the worse, forever. There are two issues that need to be addressed in relation to these concerns. First, should adults assume that if teens use error-filled language when using real-time technologies that they will use the same error-filled language in more formal written environments? Second, are all changes in language bad?

You may not realize that teens who use the real-time technologies discussed in this chapter (instant messaging and text messaging) are aware that different communications formats are used more or less successfully for different purposes. In their research on IM literacies and identities, Lewis and Fabos discovered that teens used e-mail, chat, and IM differently based on time, place, need, and purpose. In the introduction to their findings, the researchers state, "These young people were not duped by technology. Instead, they used it with a sense of purpose and informed participation that may be surprising to many adults concerned about the influence of computer-mediated communication on the lives and literacies of the younger generation" (Lewis and Fabos 2005, 482).

Adults often assume that teens simply use these technologies without thought about what they are doing and why. But research shows that is not the case. In other words, give teens credit for thinking through what makes sense in any given situation. "E-mail 'has made us definitely way more comfortable about writing, because we're doing it every day,' says Myles McReynolds, a junior at Mullen High School in Denver.... Reliance on the cipher of IM, he says, 'is just to shorten stuff up. It's not like we're doing it in real life'" (McCarroll 2005).

Having the skills to make those decisions is something you can work on with teens. Facilitate formal and informal discussions and activities that give teens opportunities to decide and articulate when the time is right to use a particular piece of communications technology.

This chapter looks at why anyone who uses real-time technologies to communicate quickly learns that grammar and spelling need to be reconsidered, how changes to language are inevitable, (and have been for thousands and thousands of years), and how using a style of writing in one context does not mean that same style will automatically be used in another context.

THE HOW AND WHY OF LANGUAGE CONVENTIONS IN REAL-TIME VIRTUAL ENVIRONMENTS

IM

Teens ... said that they view email as something you use to talk to "old people," institutions, or to send complex instructions to large groups. When it comes to casual written conversation, particularly when talking with friends, online instant messaging is clearly the mode of choice for today's online teens. (Lenhart, Madden, and Hitlin 2005, ii)

WHAT IS IM?

IM stands for Instant Messaging, a technology that allows you to know when others on your IM friends list (called a buddy list) are online. If one of your friends/buddies is online, you can click on their name in your IM program, send them a message, and talk in real time. Most IM programs allow for several people to talk to each other all at once in what is a text-based version of a conference call. Many IM programs have a save feature, so if you have been IMing with someone you can save a transcript of the IM to refer back to at a later time. Popular IM programs include AOL Messenger (http://www.aim.com/), Yahoo! Messenger (http://messenger.yahoo.com/), and MSN Messenger (http://messenger.msn.com/).

Some programs also allow subscribers to use microphones and speakers to instant message with their voice instead of with text. These programs use what is called VOIP (Voice Over Internet Protocol) to enable users to talk to each other via an Internet connection. A popular VOIP program is Skype (http://www.skype.com/).

IM is far from new, but its popularity with teens continues to grow, as the Pew Internet in American Life Project report, quoted at the opening of the IM section, demonstrates. Teens see a difference, as noted previously, between technologies and techniques used in casual vs. formal conversation. IM is for informal conversation, and e-mail is for much more formal communication. Teens appreciate IM because it allows them to multitask, to stay in touch with friends and family easily, and to exchange photos and other documents in real time.

Consider the fact that IM provides an easy way to keep in touch with family and friends. A few years ago a mother of a college student noted that her daughter remained in touch with her closest high-school friends, even though the tight-knit group of young women graduated from high school almost four years previously and each attended a different college or university. As the mother continued to talk about the relationship of the four women, it became apparent that these four communicated with each other regularly through IM. When one of the girls was happy, frustrated, angry, or sad she was quickly and easily able to connect with the others. She didn't need to rely solely on new friends who had to learn her ways and whims. She was able to continue to gain support from a group of peers with whom she felt extremely comfortable and safe and had a long and positive history.

This story is an excellent example of what makes IM a medium of choice for many teens. Friendships grow stronger and last over time. "All writing is socially mediated, but the social aspects of IM are writ large. Indeed, the maintenance of social relationships has been found

Online Teens' Communication Choices						
When you want to ____, do you usually use the phone, email, instant messaging, or text messaging?						
	Phone	**Email**	**IM**	**Text Messaging**	**Face-to-Face**[a]	**None/Other Method**
Have a quick conversation with a friend that you see on a regular basis	59%	5%	26%	7%	2%	*%
Talk with a friend about something really serious or important	74	6	9	3	7	1
Have a private conversation with someone that you don't want anyone else to find out about	60	9	18	6	6	1

Figure 2.1 Pew Internet & American Life Project: Parents & Teens 2004 Survey

Source: Pew Internet & American Life Project: Parents & Teens 2004 Survey (October/November 2004). Reprinted with permission.

to be a central function of online communication networks in general, both for the purpose of sustaining close friendships and for establishing and maintaining casual ties" (Lewis and Fabos 2005, 475).

There are also stories of teens who IM with friends and classmates while working on homework. Of course some of the conversation is not related to homework, but there are definitely portions of time when one of the teens asks another for a reminder of what an assignment is all about, asks for ideas on how to complete the assignment, or asks for help in a general or specific way. The ability to do more than one thing at the same time comes naturally to many teens who have grown up in a world where using technology to learn and communicate is the norm. Using IM to hang out with friends while doing homework is part of that normal world. And ultimately, it's no different from the way friends hang out doing homework at the library or at someone's house. It simply makes use of the technology to accomplish the hanging out.

Teens use IM to exchange photos, music, and other files and by so doing are required to use a variety of modes of communication and literacies. They listen, read, view, and converse all at the same time in order to exchange ideas with friends. As another form of multitasking, this exchange of content requires teens to think in several dimensions while keeping a conversation going. It's not easy to do, and one of the reasons adults aren't comfortable with teens communicating in this way is that many adults don't have the skills teens do to successfully facilitate and mediate this style of communication.

"... IM motivates young people to engage in decoding, encoding, interpretation, and analysis, among other literacy processes ..." (Lewis and Fabos 2005, 473). Among the findings of Louis and Fabos' influential study on IM literacy practices was the teen use of visual as well as text-based practices in order to get their message across. For example, teens used different fonts, colors, and sizes in order to give their IM messages emotions. In this way teens combine visual and text literacies in order to get ideas across and decode messages from others.

When thinking about the way teens use IM to communicate with peers, family, and others, remember that it's not simply about the language used in the communication. Communicating via IM cannot be placed into black and white categories of bad grammar vs. good grammar. While using informal language associated with technology (such as LOL—laughing out loud) and not worrying about misspellings is indeed an aspect of IM conversations, it's a result of the style of conversation inherent to the medium and should not be an indictment of the literacy skills of the people doing the communicating.

If you consider the way language is used in IM, it's clear that it's a reflection of the medium and not of teen literacy skills. As a matter of fact, teens who IM might be thought to have higher literacy skills than adults who don't IM. Teens are managing a large flow of information coming and going in an IM environment and are inventing methods for accomplishing success. That's quite a feat. How many 40+ year olds can do that easily?

Text Messaging

WHAT IS TEXT MESSAGING?

Sometimes known as texting, text messaging refers to sending short text-based messages from cell phone to cell phone. SMS (short message system) is another form of texting that makes it possible for messages to go from phone to computer or computer to phone. For example, if a teen sends a text message to Google to find out a fact or definition, that's really an SMS message because the text goes from the teen's cell phone to a Google computer (where the answer is uncovered) and then the answer is sent as a text message back to the teen's phone. While text messages cannot exceed 160 characters, computer software programs that work with SMS make it possible to send longer messages from a computer to a cell phone. The software breaks the one message into several messages, none of which exceed the 160 character limit.

According to the Pew Internet in American Life Project, sending text messages increases with the age of the teen. Seventeen percent of the 12-year-olds surveyed send text messages, while 54 percent of the 17-year-olds surveyed said that they sent text messages. The Pew Report also found that teenage girls text message more than boys and that some of those surveyed noted that barriers to texting do exist, including the cost of sending messages and incompatibilities among service providers (Lenhart, Madden and Hitlin 2005, 37).

However, even though teens note barriers to text messaging use, there is an important trend that may have an impact in the removal of those barriers. That's the use of text messaging by corporations—including publishers and other media outlets—to connect with customers and potential customers. For example:

- Teens can join Teen People Mobile by dialing TXTTP on their cell phones. Once registered, participants receive text message updates on magazine special offers and news about people in *Teen People*.

- Reality TV shows such as *The Apprentice* and *American Idol* give viewers (teens and adults) the chance to vote for their favorite contestant via text messaging. Voting for *American Idol* in 2005 broke U.S. text messaging records. "Cingular Wireless has announced that the fourth season of *American Idol* resulted in over 41.5 million text messages being sent during the show's 12-week voting period. Compared to last season, this year's text messaging totals were triple the volume recorded in 2004" (Osborne 2005).

- Sports teams and stores are getting on the text messaging bandwagon as well in order to sell their products and provide information to fans and customers (Maney 2005).

The commercial uses of text messaging require that teens receive messages via their cell phones. That means they need to be able to read the messages and, if need be, to respond. Of course that's different from being the originator of the text message and communicating with friends and family using texting. In fact, many teens are also using text messaging to communicate with family—they let their parents know if they are going to be late getting home, are staying at a friend's house for dinner, and so on. Teens also use text messaging to communicate when a computer isn't available. For example, a teen can send a text message to a friend while traveling with family in a car or while sitting at the dinner table. That teen doesn't have to turn on a computer, wait for it to boot-up, and connect to the Internet. All a teen needs is to have a cell phone with text messaging services, to turn on the phone, and to start typing.

Remember the close-knit group of girls discussed earlier in this chapter who kept in touch throughout college? Text messaging expands the access the girls have to each other in ways that IM does not. Imagine if one of those girls just broke up with her boyfriend. She wouldn't have to wait to get to her dorm room to let the others know. She could simply send a text message right from where she was after the breakup and pass on the news. If at least one of the other girls is available, her support system is instantaneously available. And, because she isn't using voice technology, she can be more private when talking about the breakup if doing so in a public place.

The language used in text messages is the same as that used in IMing. The screen on which the message is sent and received is smaller. There is a limit to the number of characters that can be included in a text message (as mentioned in the What is Text Messaging section) but the style and language used transfers between forms seamlessly. In other words the same literacies that are needed and used in IM are also used in text messaging.

Supporting IM and Texting Literacies in Libraries and Classrooms

Chat reference service has been available in many libraries for several years. But over the past few years, librarians have reconsidered the interface they use for chat reference and have started to realize that IM and texting are useful tools to use to provide service that meet the interests and abilities of those they serve—of every age.

Regarding the teen audience in particular, remember that a large number of teens IM on a regular basis. That means they have their IM software open and available any time they are at the computer. Many teens also have cell phones. They carry their phones with them wherever they go and use the phone to text or call friends or family. It makes sense that librarians serving teens incorporate the technologies used by the age group to support their needs, while at the same time helping them to expand and enhance reading and writing literacies.

IM Literacies in the Library and Classroom

I don't know of a single public library that doesn't have a hard time bringing middle and high schoolers into the library, nor do

I know of a single public library that wouldn't want to do a better job at providing services for this age group. So in addition to trying to bring teens into the library, let's also bring the library to the teens. Enter stage left: Instant Messaging Reference (IMR). (Houghton 2005, 192)

TRILLIAN

One of the barriers to providing IM service in libraries is the requirements of IM software—Yahoo! and AOL, for example. Each program can only IM with those using the same software. That means that if a library selects Yahoo!, for example, as their IM service, then if a teen uses a different piece of software for IM, the library won't be able to IM with that teen. Trillian is a software product that makes the incompatibility problems disappear. Libraries use Trillian as an IM aggregator, and as a result, once Trillian is set up, the librarians can communicate with any IM software a teen uses.

Trillian URL: http://www.ceruleanstudios.com/

IM reference is a logical extension of a library's reference services. But librarians and teachers should not stop at IM reference for teens. Literacy, information, and social connections are bound to occur via IM conversations between librarians and teens for a variety of other purposes. Consider using IM technology for the following library functions:

Readers' Advisory

Why not set up a readers' advisory IM service that is devoted entirely to connecting teens to leisure reading materials? Publicize the fact that teens can IM the librarian to talk about favorite books and to get advice on what to read next. Set up specific IM hours for different types of readers' advisories. For example, Thursday afternoons might be devoted to a readers' advisory for manga lovers.

Gift Giving

Why not have an IM gift-suggestion service for holidays and birthdays? Let teens know that librarians are on call during certain hours of the day to talk about the best new book, CD, or DVD to buy friends or family on special occasions. Teens looking for suggestions will have to provide information about friend and family likes and dislikes in writing, thereby using text literacy skills.

Youth Participation

Libraries might also promote youth participation via IM. Why not extend readers' advisory services by having teens host a library IM readers' advisory service for other teens. The project would require that teens write guidelines for the service—thereby enhancing their reading and writing skills—and then make them responsible for talking to peers, via IM, about good books to read, gifts to give, and so on.

Study Groups

It's possible to have more than one person in an IM session, so teachers might use IM as a way to promote study groups among classmates. Since most IM programs allow for saving the IM transcript, the teacher can ask study group partners or teams to save session transcripts and bring them into class. A teacher might have students review the transcripts and rewrite them in non-IM speak as a way to discuss different ways of communicating based on situation and audience. Or the teacher might have students read the transcripts aloud in order to facilitate conversation about oral vs. written communication.

CAMPFIRE

Campfire is a Web-based program that makes it easy to set up a chat room. Once you register at the Campfire site, for free, you can start a number of rooms in which up to four people can chat at the same time. (Low-cost versions of the software allow for more people to chat at once.)

The rooms can be made private so that only those you invite can join in the chat. The software also saves transcripts, so it's easy to go back to review chats and find information previously discussed.

Give it a try by signing up at http://www.campfirenow.com/.

Texting Literacies in the Library and Classroom

Texting shouldn't be ignored as teachers and librarians think about how to support teen literacy needs via technology. Once again, an obvious use of the technology is in reference service, and libraries are already integrating text messaging into reference.

Commercial examples of reference service via text messaging are seen in Google and Yahoo's services. Searching capabilities vary when texting these search tools, but between the two it's possible to find out the definition of a word, basic information about a topic (for example, the population of the United States), weather information, movie times and locations, or where the nearest store or restaurant of a particular type is located. Since these services already exist on these search engines there is no reason for librarians to replicate that simple messaging service (SMS).

However, librarians and teachers can think of other services to provide teens who are walking around the school, their home, or the mall with their cell phone in hand.

New Book Notices

Why can't libraries send notices of new books to teens via text messaging? Have teens sign up for mobile new-book notifications and send a text message when a new book by an author or in a particular genre is available in the library. In the text message make it possible for the teen to contact the library to reserve or place the item on hold and you've got a great service going. Of course these notices don't have to be available only for books. Teens might sign up for program notifications, weekly searching tips, book reviews, and so on.

Homework Support/Reminders

Imagine a teen walking around the mall and all of a sudden realizing that he has an assignment due tomorrow and he can't remember what it is. Can he text message his teacher to ask her what the assignment is? Maybe. Or maybe there's a text message number for the school system or individual school. A teen sends a message to the number from the mall, includes teacher and grade, and in a minute or so gets a response about upcoming assignments. This could even be a library service in which teachers and librarians collaborate to collect assignment information and send it out when a teen is in need.

Youth Participation

As with IM support for teens, if librarians and teachers provide opportunities for teens to manage text messaging services for their peers, the literacy benefits will be great. Teens might be responsible for writing the messages that go out, determining guidelines and policies for the services, and for responding to requests for help. Google has a wallet-size tip sheet (available at http://www.google.com/sms/tips.pdf) on using its SMS services. Teens might create the same type of resource for libraries and schools that start texting services. Imagine the literacy benefits inherent in the creation of that type of tool.

ADVANCEMENT, NOT DECLINE

You have now seen that two of the communications technologies teens use have the potential to improve rather than hinder their text-based literacies. IM and texting require a variety of skills including those related to reading and writing. "Though plenty of adults grumble about e-mail and instant-messaging (IM), and the text messages that send adolescent thumbs dancing across cell phone keypads, many experts insist that teenage composition is as strong as ever—and that the proliferation of writing, in all its harried, hasty forms, has actually created a generation more adept with the written word" (McCarroll 2005).

It's hard to believe, but IM and chat are actually two of the oldest Internet technologies around. We'll take a look at the newer technologies of blogs, wikis, and podcasts in the next chapter and see how these newer tools provide more examples of how teens practice and gain literacy skills online and how librarians and teachers can integrate those skills into the work that they do for and with teens.

3

Out There for the World: Blogs, Wikis, Podcasts

> You read a lot when you blog, and you use other people's words all the time, and instead of writing out a citation in a form that many students find very complex, you link to the Web site where you found the words. This is a writing environment that can help students learn how to connect to the ideas of others while being explicit about the connections they are making. (Walker 2005, 116)

When teens blog, they read and write. That's pretty obvious. When teens use wikis, they read and write. That's pretty obvious too. What about podcasting, however; is there reading and writing literacy associated with that? Absolutely. When teens create their own podcasts they might write notes or outlines for a script. Many podcasts have blog companions, so teen podcasters are writing about their casts on those blogs. And if teens listen to podcasts they are likely to visit the cast Web site to read more, find links to sites mentioned, and perhaps write a comment or note to the podcaster. Blogs, wikis, and podcasts provide a virtual literacy feast.

SUBSCRIBING TO BLOGS, WIKIS, AND PODCASTS WITH RSS

RSS stands for Really Simple Syndication or Rich Site Survey. One of the easiest ways to understand RSS is to think about a syndicate. A syndicate is made up of a group of people, or organizations, that all agree to take part in an activity together. A television syndicate is a group of stations that purchase the right to air specific programs. Shows that go into syndication are available for this purchase.

In the Web world, syndication refers to Web-based content that anyone can subscribe to in order to get updated information on a designated topic. In this instance the syndicate is the group of people that subscribe to the RSS feed in order to keep up-to-date. Blogs and podcasts usually have RSS feeds associated with them so that readers can be automatically informed when the blogger submits a new post or a new podcast is available. But other Web-based content providers also have RSS feeds. These include newspapers, magazines, wikis, and library catalogs and databases. Google provides RSS feeds for its news services, and database and library catalog vendors are starting to provide them as well.

To subscribe to an RSS feed the user needs to use a piece of software or Web-based tool that aggregates and displays the information available on the Web site or blog, podcast, or wiki that is subscribed to. Read more about how RSS feeds work, and what they are, in Will Richardson's *RSS Quick Start Guide for Educators* available at http://www. weblogg-ed.com/rss_for_ed.

Not only is reading and writing literacy an essential component of these various technologies, but inherent in each is the ability to publish for the world to see. All of the technologies can be used to create personal private spaces, or they can be used to connect to dozens, hundreds, or thousands of others. The ability to publish content for world consumption has a direct connection to teen literacy interests and skills. In this chapter we'll look at how teens read, write, think, and create with blogs, wikis, and podcasts and consider the impact the global nature of these technologies has on teen literacy skills.

TEEN BLOGGERS

WHAT IS A BLOG?

The word blog is short for Weblog. Weblogs started out as Web-based journals; an online tool that gave anyone the ability to easily create Web pages with content about topics in which they were interested. As the interest in blogging grew, more and more people started blogs that were more than personal journals. There are blogs on a wide variety of topics; and newspapers, TV networks, and magazines have incorporated the technology into their Web sites in order to expand the presence of their authors and reporters.

There is a host of free and fee-based blogging software available. This software makes it fairly easy to set up a template for a blog and start writing. When creating a blog entry using one of these software tools the process is not much different from creating a document with Microsoft Word.

See appendix A for resources that can help you get started blogging.

Charlotte is a teenager in southeastern Massachusetts. She keeps a blog on Live Journal—one of the most popular blogging tools used by teens—and updates it regularly. Figure 3.1 is a screenshot of Charlotte's blog from early January 2006. When you look at Charlotte's blog you'll see that her posts include the music she is listening to when she is writing the post, how she is feeling at the moment, and information on her day and/or her life. Sometimes her posts include answers to quizzes. Sometimes her posts are only a sentence or two. Sometimes her posts are longer reflections on what's going on in her life. What's clear from reading Charlotte's blog is that it is all hers. She owns it. She decides when and what to write.

Public Blogging

Blogging is a public and private matter for anyone who takes it up. Teens might blog in school and they might blog for their own personal purposes, like Charlotte. When writing a personal blog the blogger can

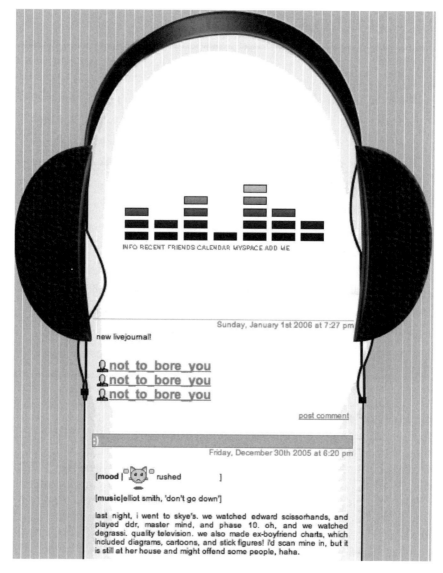

INFO RECENT FRIENDS CALENDAR MYSPACE ADD ME

Sunday, January 1st 2006 at 7:27 pm

new livejournal!

not to bore you
not to bore you
not to bore you

post comment

:)

Friday, December 30th 2005 at 6:20 pm

[mood | rushed]

[music|elliot smith, 'don't go down']

last night, i went to skye's. we watched edward scissorhands, and
played ddr, master mind, and phase 10. oh, and we watched
degrassi. quality television. we also made ex-boyfriend charts, which
included diagrams, cartoons, and stick figures! i'd scan mine in, but it
is still at her house and might offend some people, haha.

Figure 3.1 Sunday Morning Blog.

decide if the content is going to be available for the world to see. When
writing a blog for a classroom a teen might be required to create a public blog space that is available at least to the teacher and maybe to classmates as well. Yet, whether the blog is totally personal or school-based,
its author decides what is published for others to read and what is not.

Think about that for a minute. In previous decades anyone who wrote a journal knew that what was written down was only intended for the eyes of the person doing the writing. As a matter of fact, many pieces of fiction and movies center around the reading of a private journal by someone who shouldn't have done that reading. The key is found. The journal isn't locked.

Today, blogs like Charlotte's (and the many others who link to and comment on Charlotte's blog) are completely public for the world to read. Teens aren't keeping secret some of their innermost thoughts. What is the outcome of writing for a public audience? One outcome is that a teenager might be telling something that would make him or her vulnerable to a dangerous situation. Another is that a teen might be saying something threatening to others or be exposing self-destructive thoughts. What do adults do about that? Tell the teen not to blog? That, of course, isn't the answer. Instead, adults must teach teens what it takes to be safe when blogging.

STAYING SAFE WITH BLOGS, WIKIS, AND PODCASTS

The first thing to remember when talking about keeping teens safe in a digital environment is that it's not the technology that makes teens unsafe. It's what one does with the technology that causes risky situations. So it's not the fact that teens blog and use wikis and podcast that is dangerous. It's that others might take advantage of teens who do those things that presents risk.

That being the case, it's your responsibility as an adult to make sure that teens have the experience and critical thinking skills necessary to make smart decisions about what they do when using digital communications tools. That means we shouldn't tell teens not to use the tools, but teach them how to use the tools wisely.

Don't be afraid to talk to teens about what is and isn't safe. Ask teens what they actually do in order to be safe online. Listen to what teens say, and then talk with them about ways to be even safer. Don't assume that teens are acting stupidly in ways that could result in some kind of harm to themselves while blogging and so forth. They often know a lot more than adults give them credit for. Work with teens to help them be safe. That way they will know how to act when out in the world on their own.

Beyond issues of safety there are several positive literacy implications for teens who create personal or school-related blogs. In her article on Weblogs in a university classroom, Jill Walker writes, "As my blogging students realised that their writing was actually being read by other students and even by people outside the university, their writing changed" (Walker 2005, 115). Walker is not the only educator who noticed a change in student writing when it becomes public. As a matter of fact, as a part of the writing process promoted in many school systems, publishing is an end result of the process for this very reason. Publication makes the writing process more meaningful and thereby more interesting to the student. A sixth-grade student said it very well. "Because we are encouraged to go public as writers, the students in my class know that there's a greater world of writing beyond our classroom. We know that we can be part of this world if we find our own voices and our own perspectives, and send them off to make a difference" (Irving, Janney, Jordan, et al. 2004, 21).

So it's really just common sense that blogging would have the same impact on teen writing as that seen with publishing in more traditional formats. When the writing becomes meaningful in a larger context the care and commitment to that writing becomes greater.

Blogger Identity

Rebecca Blood, the blogger of Rebecca's Pocket, made another observation about the impact of writing for large groups in her post on the history of blogging. She wrote, "Shortly after I began producing Rebecca's Pocket I noticed two side effects I had not expected. First, I discovered my own interests. I thought I knew what I was interested in, but after linking stories for a few months I could see that I was much more interested in science, archaeology, and issues of injustice than I had realized. More importantly, I began to value more highly my own point of view. In composing my link text every day I carefully considered my own opinions and ideas, and I began to feel that my perspective was unique and important" (Blood 2000).

Consider what Blood is saying in terms of a teen's need to make sense of his or her personal identity. By giving teens the chance to write about what they are interested in at a particular moment in time, to link to other sites and information that connects with their interests, and then to comment on that in their own writing, blogs give teens an enormous opportunity to discover who they are. This can be seen in Charlotte's blog as well. In her December 26, 2005, blog she wrote, "rereading old journal entries … i definitely have changed a lot. i can't pinpoint it. but i can just see it. i hate who i used to be. i guess that's the problem with changing. you look at what you used to be like and shudder in disgust. and i'm sure in the future i'll look back on the me of whatever day it is right now and i'll wonder how anyone could ever put up with me. *sigh*" (Charlotte, 2005).

Of course one might get caught up in the use of lowercase in Charlotte's post about 2005. But, read what she writes without focusing on the grammar. Charlotte analyzes poignantly who she was and who she is becoming. She uses evocative language "shudder in disgust." She is letting readers into her world. And, it's her world, not that of anyone else. She has the right to write i and not I in her post to describe what she's thinking and feeling. If she were writing a research paper for her high-school English class it would be a different story. But, she's not. She's writing her personal journal. So "I" can be "i" as much as Charlotte wants.

Saying Something Meaningful

The second part of Blood's post talks about how she began to realize that her own opinions mattered and that her unique perspective was important. How does a teen get that affirmation through a blog? Two ways: through the trackbacks that others might set up to the teen's blog and posts and through the comments that someone writes related to a particular post.

A trackback is the way bloggers let each other know about references between blogs. For example, Charlotte might write a comment on her blog that relates to something she read on someone else's blog. Instead of commenting on that other person's blog Charlotte can send a trackback to the other blog to let the owner know that the blog was commented on.

Imagine a teen who writes a blog about the things in which he or she is interested. One day that teen starts to get trackbacks. Those trackbacks not only demonstrate that others are reading the blog, but that those reading the blog feel it has value in some way. In most cases, that would spur the teen on to write more and to continue writing in a way that connects to readers.

Comments have the same powerful validation for teen blog writers. When someone comments on a teen's blog, that person is saying that the post being commented on had worth and sparked interest. But not only do comments show value in terms of the original blog, they also give teens another chance to communicate in writing. When a teen writes a comment on someone else's blog, that teen needs to write the comment in such a way as to make sense to anyone who reads the blog and the comments—including the blog author and general readers. The same positive reinforcement for writing comments applies as it does for writing original blogs. The comments are published for the world to see, and in turn, the comments the commenter generates can show the value and worth of the thoughts of the commenter.

AUTHOR BLOGS/LIBRARY BLOGS

Libraries, librarians, and authors have set up blogs in order to connect with users and readers and as a way to give users and readers the chance to comment on what's going on at the library or with an author. Some examples include:

AUTHORS

Holly Black
http://blackholly.livejournal.com/
Libba Bray
http://libba-bray.livejournal.com/
Sarah Dessen
http://writergrl.livejournal.com/
Neil Gaiman
http://www.neilgaiman.com/journal/
Gail Giles
http://notjazz.livejournal.com/
John Green
http://www.sparksflyup.com/weblog.php
Brent Hartinger
http://brentsbrain.livejournal.com/
Pete Hautman
http://petehautman.com/whatsnew.html
Megan McCafferty
http://www.meganmccafferty.com/retroblogger/

LIBRARIES AND LIBRARIANS

Alternative Teen Services
   http://yalibrarian.com/
Framingham Public Library YA Blog
   http://fplya.blogspot.com/
Parma Public Library for Teens
   http://pplya.edublogs.org/
PDL Teen Blog
   http://teenblog.plymouthlibrary.org/
Pop Goes the Library
   http://www.popgoesthelibrary.com/

Reading in a Blogger's World

This discussion on blogging focuses primarily on the literacy of writing and how that is supported by online journaling via blogs. However, note that reading is also a key component of successful blogging. Teen bloggers read the comments left by others on their blogs, and of course those who read a teen's blog are . . . reading. It is likely, also, that the teen who writes a blog reads his or her original posts before publishing in order to determine clarity and tone of voice. Going back to the idea of the importance of publishing for the world to read, a teen blogger wants to make sure that what is on his or her blog is written in a way that will make sense to the audience of readers. That requires reading.

Reading the Audience

When setting up a blog, a teen needs to think about who will read the postings. A personal blog that is mostly an online journal that friends and others might read regularly requires a different look and tone then a blog that is intended to act as a way for a group of teens to inform local community members of a particular cause or interest. When setting up and maintaining a blog, when writing posts on the blog, and when replying to comments, a teen blogger needs to think about the audience. And the style and tone of the blog is determined based on the audience. Teens therefore have to know how to write and present information for a particular audience.

If you look at the screenshot from Charlotte's blog again (figure 3.1) you'll see a definite style to the blog. Charlotte tells us a lot about herself based on the way the blog looks. Seeing headphones and volume bars on the blog would suggest that Charlotte really likes music. Other teens who are also music lovers will be drawn in by the look of Charlotte's blog. If you browse teen blogs on Live Journal or other blogging sites, you'll see that a lot can be inferred about the blogger from the look of their blog. For example, anime and/or manga lovers integrate their own drawings of characters into their blog designs. The audience for these blogs is definitely the teen himself or herself along with others who have the same likes and dislikes.

Teen blogs created for schools and libraries don't usually have the same individual look as those created by teens for personal use. However, in all instances, those creating the blog need to consider audience and purpose in order to determine content and tone. As an educator, you can use teen blogging as an opportunity to talk about how one decides what the best way to present information is. It's an opportunity to speak with teens about how medium and message connect along with the importance of selecting the right look, feel, and words in order to get ideas across successfully. Teens are often thinking about "me." But when writing for the world—particularly when it's for a school or library purpose—the teens need to think beyond themselves. Blogs present a great opportunity for supporting teens in their understanding of the world beyond me.

Blog Integration

Taking into account all of the literacy aspects of blogging discussed above, consider the following specific classroom and library use examples.

Reaction Blog

There are a lot of times in a teen's life that provide opportunity for reaction. These include reacting to what they read, hear, and see in their day-to-day lives. Each teen in your library or classroom might set up a blog in which they get to react to what is going on around them. It might be a blog specifically to react to assignments and projects in a specific subject area. It might be a blog to specifically react to a type of media. Or it might be a blog to react to the teen's world in general.

Comment Connections

The commenting feature of blogs is a powerful tool for teens, librarians, and teachers to use. Think about the comments as a basis for reaction to content more than as a chance to take part in a conversation. That means that you can post an idea, a provocative question, or the name of a TV show and ask teens to comment on what you posted. If successful, the comments will provide an overview for you and the teens of reactions on a particular topic.

News Blog

A blog is a perfect journalistic tool. Use a blog as a place for teens to report on different interests areas. Teens might write articles on books, authors, curriculum topics, things happening in the community, and so on. Other teens could comment on the articles and provide suggestions via the comments for future article topics.

WIKIS

Regardless of how educators feel about the potential of wikis—and the hesitancy many teachers feel is understandable—one thing remains certain. The collaborative environment that wikis facilitate can teach students much about how to work with others, how to create community, and how to operate in a world where the creation of knowledge and information is increasingly becoming a group effort. (Richardson, 2005, 20)

WHAT IS A WIKI?

Wiki is a term that is used both for a piece of software and for an interactive Web site people use to collaborate online. The software is called wiki and the Web site that people create with the software is called a wiki.

Wiki users create content on a Web site, and others can edit, change, and add to that content. In most instances, a wiki can be set up so that either it's open to the general public or it's private and only those who are a part of the wiki community can collaborate within the wiki space.

See appendix A for a list of tools you can use to set up a wiki.

There's no doubt about it—wikis get a lot of bad press. In late 2005, two news stories gained national attention as potential problems with wikis were exposed. Both stories had to do with biographical content on Wikipedia (http://www.wikipedia.org). The first was an article on John

Seigenthaler Sr. that suggested that Mr. Seigenthaler had been involved in the assassinations of John and Robert Kennedy. Seigenthaler, a journalist, did work for Robert Kennedy, and he wrote in *USA Today,* when the Wikipedia incident occurred, about his annoyance with the online article and its author (Seelye 2005).

The second incident involved Adam Curry, an MTV V-J in the 80s currently credited with being one of the "fathers" of podcasting. Curry was found to have edited portions of the Wikipedia article on podcasting so that his role in its invention was more prominent. After it was discovered that Curry made the changes, he apologized for what he claimed was an error, and the entry was revised (Terdiman 2005).

Wiki Pros and Cons

In each of these instances both the negative consequences and positive aspects of an open community such as Wikipedia are seen. On the negative side, the ease of and public access to content revision can be problematic. At Wikipedia anyone can write anything, and the person doing the writing doesn't have to own up to their edits, additions, or changes. But at the same time the nature of the wiki community means that errors and authors are usually uncovered. In the Curry incident, it was discovered that someone from a specific IP address was making changes to the podcasting entry, and that address was found to be Adam Curry's. In the Seigenthaler example, the author of the changes in the entry stepped forward when he discovered how upset Seigenthaler was as a result of the entry. People sometimes choose to log in to Wikipedia in order to make sure that their entries are traceable to a particular author. But that is not required or always the case.

On the positive side, Curry and Seigenthaler have the ability to write about themselves and the events in which they have been involved. Primary sources can create and edit content that anyone has easy access to. That's pretty amazing. Another amazing piece of the wiki software is that it's possible to see a history of changes. That means that one can go back and look at the podcasting entry, for example, and see when and what changes were made and then also see when the Seigenthaler entry reverted to its form prior to the Kennedy assassination allegations. The history feature of wikis has strong connections to the writing process of editing, revising, and so on. The difference of course in a wiki is that the same person isn't always doing the editing and revising from entry point to entry point.

Writing History

The other facet of the historical perspective of wiki changes is that readers can compare entries. It's possible to select several entries from a history list and see them side-by-side. That way readers and writers gain a full understanding of revisions. This kind of history provides great opportunities for teachers and librarians to talk with teens about the how and why of revisions in writing. It's possible to see in the Wikipedia revision history that revisions come in many forms, from those related to spelling and grammar to those specifically related to content quality. Teens are likely to be better writers if they have a transparent view of a revision process via something like Wikipedia.

Beyond Wikipedia

Wikipedia may be the best-known wiki. However, Wikipedia simply makes use of a software application—wiki—in order to make content available to readers and writers. Anyone can set up a wiki and start creating content for others to work with. A wiki community can be closed, so that only those invited and with a username and password can take part in editing, revising, and so on. Or, like Wikipedia, the community can be open to anyone who wants to participate. In schools and libraries both closed and open wiki communities have a great deal of potential depending on the audience and purpose of a wiki, as you'll see in the following section.

Going back to Adam Curry, for quite a long time Curry used a blog to post information about his almost daily podcast (The Daily Source Code). At one point Curry realized that updating the content on the blog was too time consuming, so he asked his listeners for suggestions. The end result was a wiki. Now, listeners of the podcast post information on each show. That means that listeners write about the content, link to sites and people discussed, and so on. It's a community transcript and works very well for the specific need of Curry and his podcast listeners.

Teens and Wikis

What should schools and libraries be thinking about in terms of teen use of wikis and how that use supports their literacy needs? Imagine that a group of teens set up a wiki as a place to keep group notes and information about a specific project. For example, maybe a group of teens is working on a school assignment about the Middle Ages. The group might use the wiki to keep track of bibliographic sources, take notes on different aspects of the research, and create a glossary of unfamiliar

02:53, 10 December 2005 71.99.158.88 *(→Publications)*

01:16, 10 December 2005 Gamaliel *(→Publications - actually by his son, see talk)*

00:56, 10 December 2005 Katefan0 *(→References - rm reference to E&P (see previous edit))*

00:56, 10 December 2005 Katefan0 *(rm threat information erroneously attributed by E&P to Siegenthaler Sr.)*

23:02, 9 December 2005 67.84.253.123 *(→Wikipedia controversy)*

23:01, 9 December 2005 67.84.253.123 *(→Wikipedia controversy)*

22:40, 9 December 2005 Hall Monitor m *(Reverted edits by 69.205.171.21 (talk) to last version by OwenX)*

22:40, 9 December 2005 69.205.171.21 *(→Later life)*

22:39, 9 December 2005 OwenX m *(Reverted edits by 69.205.171.21 (talk) to last version by Hall Monitor)*

22:39, 9 December 2005 69.205.171.21 *(→Time as publisher)*

22:39, 9 December 2005 Hall Monitor m *(Reverted edits by 69.205.171.21 (talk) to last version by Jossifresco)*

22:39, 9 December 2005 69.205.171.21 *(→Time as publisher)*

22:38, 9 December 2005 69.205.171.21 *(→Beginnings as a reporter)*

20:45, 9 December 2005 Jossi m *(Reverted edits by 68.34.229.121 (talk) to last version by Varizer)*

20:44, 9 December 2005 68.34.229.121

17:46, 9 December 2005 Varizer *(now the section was really too long)*

17:44, 9 December 2005 Editorcch m *(Spelling)*

17:34, 9 December 2005 Kzollman m *(Reverted edits by 138.88.118.41 (talk) to last version by 65.125.73.4)*

17:32, 9 December 2005 138.88.118.41 *(Spelling of Name)*

17:27, 9 December 2005 65.125.73.4 *(I just put Robert Kennedy's full middle name.)*

16:26, 9 December 2005 213.118.47.218

16:26, 9 December 2005 213.118.47.218

16:02, 9 December 2005 Antandrus m *(Reverted edits by 81.86.125.153 (talk) to last version by Lancer9910)*

Figure 3.2 Sample Wikipedia History Screen Showing Date and Time of Change, Content of Change, and Author (if Known) of Change.

terms, and they might reflect on what they are learning. Each teen would add findings and information to the wiki whenever he or she had new information to incorporate. Each teen could revise content based on new materials uncovered. If the glossary of terms was incorporated, when a teen came across a new term, he or she could check the wiki for a definition; and if not there, when the definition is uncovered, it could be added for others to access (and perhaps revise.) There is always a record of changes and revisions so that everyone in the group will know who did what and when. (The teacher would know the same, of course.)

Teens can also create wikis on topics of personal interest—music, movies, TV, and so on. For example, a group of teens might start a wiki about favorite books and authors. Teens would write content about books and authors of their choosing and others could add and edit entries as appropriate.

An aspect of wikis that hasn't yet been discussed plays an important part within the context of teen communities getting together to write content. Wiki software includes a section for discussion. That means that anyone with access to the wiki can select the "discuss" link and talk with others about the topic of a particular entry. For example, a teen might post on the wiki information about a favorite musical group—Belle and Sebastian. Other teens can read the article and start a discussion about the information on the group. They might talk about what they like and don't like about the music. They might talk about which member of the band is their favorite and why. In other words, the content created by one teen can lead to discussion by a group of teens.

Wiki Literacies

As mentioned previously, wikis (like blogs) give teens the chance to participate in the writing process and the opportunity to publish content for a large group of readers. Often writing on a wiki is reality based. There are blogs that focus on fiction topics, of course, but the nature of a wiki—the updating and revising features—makes it particularly suitable for nonfiction writing. Through wikis teens can analyze information and learn how to decide the accuracy and validity of information. They can analyze information in order to determine what makes nonfiction writing readable and interesting. And they can use the technology to practice individually, and with others, their own writing in order to create content that is accurate and readable.

HEAR ALL ABOUT IT—PODCASTING

So far this chapter has focused on reading and writing technologies. Now it's time to turn to a technology that isn't obviously related to reading and writing—podcasting. Teens are podcasting in school, in the library, and at home. They podcast to inform others about a particular topic and to let listeners know something about their lives.

WHAT IS PODCASTING?

Podcasts are audio files uploaded to the Web for others to download. What makes a podcast different from any other audio file on the Web is that the creators of the podcast usually create audio on a regular basis. These audio files are uploaded to the Web and can be distributed via subscription. That means that someone interested in a podcast can subscribe to the cast and receive an update on their computer whenever a new audio file is available for download.

See appendix A for a list of tools to use in creating podcasts, and appendix B for information on subscribing to blogs, wikis, and podcasts.

Podcasting and Identity

Podcasting motivates me because you feel like you are telling the world about little stuff that we do. It makes you feel important and accepted. (Anderson 2005, 43)

A Google search for Martina Butler results in a wide range of hits. The most important for this discussion, however, are the links to Butler's podcast, and perhaps even more importantly, the links to stories in many major media outlets about Butler being the first teenage podcaster to secure corporate sponsorship for her podcast. Imagine how Butler feels about herself as a result of this event. It has to be empowering for a 15-year-old to not only have a podcast that a group of teens and adults listen to, but also to have at least one major corporation who thinks the work is good enough for their advertising. Beyond that, to be reported on in a variety of outlets creates an even greater sense of self-esteem and acceptance.

Podcasting, like blogging, makes it possible for teens to connect with a large audience to tell about their lives, their likes and dislikes, and so on. Along with Butler and her Emo Girl Talk podcast, there are many other teenagers using the medium to communicate with others. High-school sophomore Kristina Summerfrost calls her podcast Pod Princess. Listeners to the almost weekly Pod Princess podcast learn about life at 16 and what's hot and what's not in popular culture and find out everything from how to be more effective using Google to facts about holiday traditions.

An interesting commonality between these two podcasts—besides being created by teenage girls—is that each cast is produced in association with the teenager's father. In both instances, the teens show that they have great relationships with their fathers, as they are ready to talk about their lives in front of their parent and they are interested in spending time with their parent on such a project.

LIBRARY PODCASTS

Library podcasts for and by teens are popping up. Below are some examples.

Carnegie Library of Pittsburgh

http://www.ourmedia.org/node/228166

Cheshire Public Library

http://www.cheshirelib.org/teens/cplpodcast.htm

Hopkinton High School and Middle School

http://www.hopkintonschools.org/hhs/library/podcast.html

Lansing Public Library

http://www.lansing.lib.il.us/podcast.htm

You can find many education related podcasts at the Education Podcast Network, http://www.epnweb.org/index.php

---

Worldwide Listenership

Girls aren't the only podcasters, of course. Teens of both genders are podcasting about topics of interest. Along with podcasts about teen life in general, there are music, game, technology, and comedy podcasts, to name a few, produced by teens. Podcasters come from all over the United States and all over the globe. Similarly, listeners come from around the country and the world. Teen podcasters have maps on their sites to show where their listeners are located. For example, the Teen Podcasters Network has a map on Frappr (http://www.frappr. com/teenpodcasters) that shows where members of the network are located. Kristina Summerfrost has a map on her site that shows there are only six states from which she doesn't have listeners.

Within the literacy context, the maps that teens create and use to show listener locations bring a new component into the discussion. Kristina Summerfrost charts not just which locations are covered on her map but also those that are not included. She wants to have a listener from every state and every country included. That means she pays attention to the geography of her listeners. She looks up locations to find out where listeners are and are not. She writes about her map and which locations are still missing listeners. Reading and writing text, and reading maps are all a part of her podcasting experience.

WHAT IS A PODCATCHER?

The term podcatcher is used to describe a piece of software or Web site that you can use to catch the podcasts to which you subscribe. For example, iTunes is a podcatcher. When you find a podcast that you want to subscribe to, you subscribe via iTunes. Whenever there is a new edition of the podcast to which you subscribed, iTunes catches it and puts it in your podcast folder.

The Listening Experience

In the article "Something in the Air: Podcasting in Education" (2005) Gardner Campbell describes the life of a student who listens to podcasts as an integral part of her education experience. He describes the student, Jenny, who downloads entertainment and school-related podcasts all at the same time. He discusses how Jenny listens to a podcast produced by classmates and how listening to these class-related audio files, in which students discuss class readings, helps her to better understand text. Campbell also highlights that Jenny can listen to the podcasts on her way to breakfast and especially enjoys listening to the weekly podcast from one of her instructors in which he talks about interesting articles read during the previous week.

Giving learners the opportunity to understand content through listening is an important aspect of podcasting. It's commonly understood that people of all ages learn in different ways. For some, hearing content read aloud makes it easier to grasp meaning. The podcaster can use an expressive voice in order to help make content understandable. "I loved being able to listen to the lectures at my convenience, to be able to listen to difficult portions several times, and just hear the material again—while working out, or running other errands—and I think the value of listening to the lectures showed through with a high score on the first exam" (Flanagan and Calandra 2005, 21). A podcast listener can rewind the audio over and over again. Sometimes print learners need to reread passages in a text in order to grasp meaning. Podcasts and other forms of audio content give audio learners the same opportunity.

The Creating Experience

Podcasts can be formal, informal, or somewhere in between. The formality of the audio determines to some extent the process a teen uses to create the file. For example, at the formal end, a teen might write out an entire script for a podcast and then when recording read exactly from the script. At the informal end of the spectrum the teen might simply pick up a microphone and start talking. When talked out, the teen would be done with the podcast.

Most personal and school- or library-related podcasts fall somewhere in between the formal and informal approach to podcasting. Outlines instead of scripts are common, as are spontaneous moments of commentary. Outlining content for a podcast is an ideal way for teens to learn organizational skills and how to weave content together in a meaningful way. Outlines are required for all types of writing teens must do, from writing a research paper or a book review to a newspaper article or a book report. As teens think about the best way to put the pieces of a podcast together, they need to consider how to make transitions from content area to content area. They need to think about how the organization of the audio can have an impact on people's interest in the content.

Listening to the Pod Princess podcast one can tell that Kristina Summerfrost has a specific plan for how the content is organized. Her podcast is a good example of one that falls in the center between formality and informality. There are definitely segments of the audio that Kristina Summerfrost has written out, for example, when she talks about how to search Google effectively. But there are other parts of the podcasts that are much less scripted, for example, when she talks about what she's been doing with her friends. Pod Princess has a good flow and keeps listeners involved because of the varied presentation.

Listener Attention

As mentioned in the section of this chapter on blogs, teens need to consider who their audience is as they outline and produce a podcast. Martina Butler is podcasting for her peers who are interested in Emo music. She includes songs in the Emo style. Her organizational style is a bit less organized than that of the Pod Princess. Often she will remark on the limited content of the show, and often she giggles with friends as they talk about Degrassi Jr. High—*Next Generation,* something they recently did, or school events. An audience of other 15-year-olds will appreciate the content, tone, and style. If Martina were looking to attract a different audience, she might have to be more formal in her production. But one of the wonderful things about podcasting is that informality is fine if it fits the audience and purpose.

School and library podcasts produced by teens also run the gamut from formal to informal. An example of a school podcast that is tightly scripted is that produced by students at the East Oakland Community School in California (http://eastoakland.libsyn.com/). Each podcast includes students talking about their lives. It's fairly evident that the students involved in the project have decided exactly what they are going to talk about in each production and have scripted their commentaries. While at times the teens are obviously struggling with reading the text of their script, the podcast is an excellent example of giving teens the opportunity to talk about things that are important to them. Writing podcast scripts, reading the scripts, organizing the content, and deciding on content all give the East Oakland teens a chance to make their world known. One can assume that after producing several podcasts, these teens will become more secure in their skills and will be able to read their scripts more smoothly.

Another high-school podcast shows how informality can work as well as formality does. The Bush School Podcast (https://www.bush.edu/library/) is produced by a group of students in a program the school calls the Active Module Program (Bush School Podcasts). The second podcast produced by the teens includes an interview with a local band, interviews with school community members about a trash problem in the school cafeteria, a discussion with a guidance counselor about stress in teenage girls, and a roundtable discussion on Harry Potter.

What stands out in the Bush School podcasts are the production values. The podcasts are obviously well thought out. Students plan and organize the content, write at least an outline of what they want to cover in interviews and commentary, and determine where and how interviews will take place. Music is also integrated into all aspects of the podcast: at the opening and closing of the show and playing underneath much of voice content of the audio file.

Musical Life

Music plays a strong part in a teen's identity, and music often plays an important role in the podcasts that teens produce. As mentioned above, the Bush School podcast includes music throughout to highlight content. Martina Butler has as the main focus of her podcast a musical style. The role music can play in podcasting provides opportunities for discussion with teens about how music and sound effects can support understanding of content. As teens produce podcasts they might listen to various pieces of music and think about the emotions and thoughts different types of music elicit. They can talk with their fellow podcasters about the music and what it means to them. They can write on a blog associated with the podcast about why music for a particular podcast episode was selected. In this way, something of great interest to teens can be integrated into the medium and also used to help teens improve their literacy skills.

An important issue teens need to discuss when creating podcasts and integrating music into the audio files is that of copyright. It may seem obvious to you that teens should not simply take any song and use it in their podcasts, but it may or may not be obvious to teens. This is the perfect opportunity for librarians and teachers to remind teens about copyright and to help them understand what their options are in order not to violate copyright law. Teens might register for the Podsafe Music Network (http://music.podshow.com/), where they can find music from independent musicians that is available for use in podcasts.

PUTTING THE PIECES TOGETHER

In this chapter we have covered a lot of territory, from reading and writing with blogs and wikis, to organizing content and producing audio with podcasts. Remember that the content creation arena is moving fast, and almost every day there is an announcement about a new technology or use of technology that allows creation of digital content. Vodcasts, the video version of podcasts, are a reality, and teens are already working in that area. Stay on top of these creation technologies and consider the literacy ramifications for adolescents.

Each of the technologies discussed in this chapter enables teens to gain support for and refine their literacy skills. Each does that in some similar ways, yet there are some differences as well. For each technology tool, remember that teens' literacy skills are enhanced whenever they are able to:

- Make decisions based on a number of factors, for example, decide on the look of the blog they create in order to meet the needs of a particular audience and purpose or determine which music to use with a segment of a podcast

- Collaborate with others, as they do when building content on a wiki
- Read content, which happens on blogs and wikis and in the show notes for a specific podcast
- Write and produce content, as is accomplished by teens who work on podcasts
- Respond to content, an integral part of blogs and wikis
- Create something new, as each of the technologies discussed in this chapter enables teens to do.
- Talk to others about ideas and content, as happens when teens develop their ideas for their blogs, wikis, and podcasts and after they've read or listened to the content from a blog, wiki, or podcast.

4

Making Connections with Tagging

> Simply put, tags are important because they allow your users to generate content and classify that content in their own unique way. (Nick W. 2005)

Tagging is all about using words to categorize and describe content. As a matter of fact, a new term, folksonomy, was coined as a result of the practice of tagging in the online environment. Folksonomy combines folk and taxonomy to describe the way information is categorized, through tagging, on the Web. In this chapter we'll look at what tagging is and how it is used, and consider the direct literacy implications for teens in tagging and how librarians and teachers working with teens can integrate tagging into their programs in order to support teen literacy needs.

A KEYWORD BY ANY OTHER NAME

Keywords are nothing new. Librarians use them in cataloging and classification all the time. They use them, however, within a scientific construct that specifies what keywords to use within particular situations. Tagging takes the scientific nature out of keyword indexing and opens it up so that anyone can add a tag (a keyword or subject heading) to content. That tag can be meaningful to the tagger in a personal sense, or it can be meaningful in a global sense. For example, the library catalog subject headings used for the novel *Twilight* by Stephanie Meyer include vampires, schools, and Washington State. Those subject headings are global, as they describe the contents of the book in a general way.

A teen who tags *Twilight* on a blog or tagging Web site might use terms like vampires, scary, frightening, Robert, or cool. In this case, the use of the term vampires is exactly the same as in the subject headings in a library catalog record. The use of the word vampire in the tag describes generally what the book is about. The terms scary and frightening are personal descriptions (tags) of how the teen felt when reading the book. The person's name, Robert, could be the name of a character in the book or it could be someone the teen reader was reminded of when reading *Twilight*. Cool is what the teen thought of the book. These tags for this book are personal responses from a specific reader.

Because tagging enables personal response to content, it brings the discussion of technology and literacy to the topic of adolescent identity. The ability for a teen to tag content in a way that makes sense to him or her has a direct relationship to that teen's sense of identity. Tagging gives the teen a chance to think specifically about what the item being tagged—a book, movie, TV show, song, or magazine—means within the context of his or her own life. As teens figure out how they fit in the world, a part of that understanding comes from determining the meaning of ideas and things. Tagging gives teens the opportunity to do that through describing content.

In a conversation on identity it's important to realize that tagging in this context includes both making meaning and making connections to others with the same interests, reflections, and methods of analyzing content. In figure 4.1, the interests of Charlotte (the blogger discussed in chapter 3) are shown. These are Charlotte's tags about the things in which she is interested. Her list includes titles of TV shows and movies, names of authors, things she likes to do, ways she wants to be, and so

Interests: **146:** 1, 1984, 24, 80's music, acceptance, alice in wonderland, alternative rock, american idiot, arguments, art, australia, being happy, bill & ted, billie joe armstrong, billy elliot, blowing bubbles, blue man group, books, boston, bowling, boys, brand new, butch walker, butterfly effect, c.s. lewis, cadbury mini eggs, cartel, cats, chuck palahniuk, circa survive, cold weather, coldplay, concerts, corpse bride, creme eggs, cruises, csi, dan masterson, dane cook, danny elfman, dashboard confessional, daydreaming, death cab for cutie, differing opinions, donnie darko, drawing, dreams, duct tape, eating, edward scissorhands, emo, emotions, england, english, eternal sunshine, fall out boy, family, family guy, fight club, flowers, food, french fries, friends, fun, garden state, george orwell, girl scout cookies, green day, grey's anatomy, guitar, harry potter, hawaii, history, house, indie, ipods, jack's mannequin, johnny depp, jumping, just surrender, kissing, latin, laughing, life, literature, local bands, london, love, mae, mini coopers, mix cd's, mountain dew, movies, music, musicians, narnia, neurology, oscar wilde, painting, panic! at the disco, philosophy, phonebooth, photography, pirates of the caribbean, politics, psychology, rain, rainbows, reactions, reading, reminiscing, rock, school, shakespeare, shopping, smiles, soccer, stars, staying up late, sunsets, swimming, symbolism, text messaging, the academy is..., the beatles, the birdcage, the cadence, the nightmare before christmas, the northwood, the oc, the princess bride, the rocket summer, the simpsons, the sims, the starting line, tim burton, track, traveling, treos, trying new things, ursuline academy, vh1, weekends, weird people, writing,

Figure 4.1 Sunday Morning Blogger Interests.

forth. Charlotte, or a visitor to the site, can click on any of the tags and find a list of others who have the same interests. Then it's possible to click on that person's list and read his or her blog, and so on. Teens get to know others like themselves within this framework. Charlotte can then connect to others who have like interests. She doesn't have to be alone in her interests. Her world and identity expand as a result of tagging.

Beyond the Blog

It makes sense to tag content in a personal blog that relates specifically to a teenager's day-to-day life and the things that he or she writes about on the blog. There are also numerous sites outside of blogs that give teens the chance to tag content globally and personally outside of the "it's all about me" context. In the following section of this book we'll look at two of these resources.

Flickr

This is one of the most well known tagging sites. Flickr allows users to upload photos and describe those photos with tags. Visitors to the site can search the photo database with terms that have been used as tags in order to locate images. Because the tags are both personal and global in nature, a Flickr searcher is able to use the term "me" to locate images that others have tagged with the word "me" as a way to describe the image. It's also possible to search Flickr for a more traditional term, such as Brooklyn, and find images of people, places, and things in Brooklyn.

Thinking about searching using the term "me" is a good start when considering teen literacy connections. Someone who tags content on Flickr (or any other site) with the word "me" is obviously looking at a specific photo in a personal way. "Me" definitely describes the photo for the person who is tagging it that way, but it won't be meaningful to anyone else in exactly the same way. An important part of teen literacy skills is the ability to describe content in more than one way. This relates to the ability to connect descriptions to a particular audience and purpose. When coming up with tags for Flickr images, teens need to consider who is going to be looking at the images and what the best way is to describe those images for the people searching the database. (A Flickr user can choose to not make his or her images public. The choice of tags for nonpublic images—which might be seen just by friends and family—might be different from the choice of tags for public images.)

Within an educational context, Flickr provides significant opportunities for helping students understand literacy concepts related to description of content. For example, imagine a group of teenagers working on a project in which they determine the qualities required in order for a video game to be considered successful. Teens study examples of video games and develop a list of criteria that games should meet in order to be worth purchasing or playing. They then take photos of peers playing the various games and upload those to Flickr. As a final step they use tags to describe the content based on their criteria. In the gaming context they might upload a photo of a group playing Dance Dance Revolution (DDR) and use tags such as fast, exercise, music, customizable, and so on.

In the above example, teens use Flickr and tagging as a step towards creating a final product. Within the framework of the product and its purpose, they need to think about what tags make sense to describe the qualities of DDR that make it a good—or bad—gaming experience. They aren't simply writing tags that make sense within their own personal experience, but they are using tags that make sense in connection with an understanding of how to evaluate game quality and must use terminology that bridges the criteria developed with the capabilities provided by tagging with Flickr.

Flickr URL: http://www.flickr.com

---

43 Things

43 Things brings people together through personal goals. The front page of the site, shown in figure 4.2, provides a glimpse of recent goals people have posted. It also shows the most popular goals of the moment. Within the tagging environment, the larger a tag shows up on a list the more popular it is. (The visual representation of tags on a Web site is commonly referred to as a tag cloud.) This means that in figure 4.2 "stop procrastinating" is an extremely popular goal.

It's always possible to search 43 Things to find out goals people either are working towards or wish to accomplish, where they want to go, and where they have already visited. (43 Places is a sister site to 43 Things.) For example, a search for "library" on 43 Things returns a result list that includes the following tags: have a library, catalog my library, build my library, and go to library school. It's possible to click on an item in the result list and see how many people have that same goal. Those registered for the site can add the goal to their

189,342 people in 4,554 cities are doing 306,817 things including...

sit up straight save more money Chocolatellama wants to stop crying learn the constellations organize my photos finish a half-ironman **Learn Ruby** master English writing Graduate from university **stop procrastinating** fall in love everyday for the rest of my life!! listen better Work overseas in a third world country learn PHP start using positive affirmations daily angeljcsgurl wants to Graduate Massage Therapy College Complete a triathalon travel to Russia read all the Sandman graphic novels Learn how to remember peoples' names become a much, much better digital photographer figure out where home is Explore Brooklyn Chinatown read as many books as possible, starting with all the books I own but haven't read find a better job compile a 100-things-about-me list go to medical school girl upstairs wants to make more money live with someone i love trade referrals for a free ipod! watch every freakin' south park episode go to Europe again blog more often read war and peace live in japan for a year get my ged online for free in a day or two visit new york city See a Broadway show work for Apple Christina wants to interview Ben Gibbard declutter my life salsa like a Cuban **stop biting my nails** Kiss a stranger Love without fear Learn to whistle with my fingers stay in touch with friends Take a road trip across the USA organize photographs into albums vti wants to get a gmail invite Sponsor a child **Quit Smoking** have children learn not let people take advantage of me Excercise more **be more patient** learn how to play chess Host a dinner party find my father drive a race car get better at speaking in public **Buy a House** Nikki wants to learn to play Roma-style violin **Skydive** watch gone with the wind

Figure 4.2 43 Things Tag Cloud.

own list and then write about the goal and list tags for the goal. For example, in the listing for "I want to go to library school," tags include mlis, mls, librarianship. Members of the site can also send "cheers" to people with particular goals and of course receive "cheers" on their own goals.

What does 43 Things have to do with literacy? As with Flickr, the site gives teens the chance to describe content based on either personal or global criteria. Because a teen can go beyond simply tagging a goal at 43 Things to write about their goals, the site takes the concept one step further. Imagine a group of teens working on a project about heroes of the twentieth century. A part of the project might be to determine the achievements of the heroes that a teen might want to achieve him or herself. The teens could list the goals, explain why they too have those goals, and also tag the goals so that they are succinctly described for others to uncover. In this example a teen is writing in multiple levels and formats in order to get ideas across.

As mentioned above, 43 Things has a sister site called 43 Places. This site uses the same framework as 43 Things, writing goals for places one wants to go or writing about a place already visited. Using 43 Places to enhance teen literacy gives teens a chance to describe, both via tags and via longer entries, locations of importance to them in some way. Imagine a teen getting ready to go on a trip that he or she has been looking forward to. The site 43 Places is a perfect opportunity to describe why the trip is going to be worthwhile and what specifically the teen wants to do while traveling. The tags a teen creates for entries on 43 Places are opportunities to concisely highlight aspects of the trip that are most important and information about particular locations.

The combination of full and concise descriptions that is possible on sites like 43 Places and 43 Things is a boon to teen literacy skills.

---

43 Places URL: http://www.43places.com/

43 Things URL: http://www.43things.com/

Out of the Chaos

> A folksonomy is nearly useless for searching out specific, accurate information, but that's beside the point. (Sterling 2005)

From the traditional librarian's standpoint, it may seem that tagging is simply a way to create digital chaos. Maybe in some instances it is. But it's important to think about folksonomies as part of a larger structure. In a post on his blog in early 2005, Lou Rosenfeld wrote that there are many different ways to organize information and that folksonomies and more formal structures, used in library catalogs for example, are just two ways to help people find and organize information (Rosenfeld 2005). Rosenfeld went on to say, "In fact, it's exciting to consider how these two approaches might fit together and function as a whole. Neither works especially well on its own: controlled vocabularies often miss out on input from content authors and become rigid, stale, and distant from the vernacular of users; folksonomies will begin to break down for the reasons mentioned above."

It's up to librarians and teachers to think about how to work with teens to help them understand the interplay between the different categorization models and determine how the structures can work together to enhance literacy experiences. Recently discussions on blogs and within the library community focused on integrating tagging capabilities into integrated library systems. This means that a teen would be able to find items in the library catalog either using traditional subject heading terminology or using tags that librarians, or a teen's peers, have added to the record. While the tags of peers might create a chaotic environment, the combination of structured terminology with folk terminology will help guarantee teens find what they are looking for.

This example would also allow teens to find out what topics and types of content are of most interest to peers. A tag cloud, such as the one shown in figure 4.2, of tags entered into library catalog records would give teens the chance to see what's hot and what's not. Any teenager could look at the tag cloud and see whether or not his or her interests are represented. The teen might be inspired to do some tagging in order to make sure his interests are represented. That would require that he or she find materials and determine which tags work best to describe materials of import.

The tag cloud provides teens with an opportunity to chart trends and interests over a period of time. Imagine that a group of teens develops a schedule for checking a library's most popular tags. At designated times the teens take a screen shot of the tag cloud and keep up with the practice over a predetermined period of time. At the end of the time period the teens look at the various screen shots and begin to consider and draw conclusions about trends, world and local events, and such from the ebb and flow of items shown in a tag cloud. It's an entirely new way to create time lines and a way that would directly connect with teenagers' day-to-day lives.

INFORMATION LITERACY CAN'T BE IGNORED

The primary goal of this book is to look at how the text-based literacy skills of teens are changed and enhanced by current technology and technology trends. However, when considering a topic such as tagging, it can't be ignored that information literacy is a key component of teen use of tagging technologies. Since tagging is all about categorization of information—either from a global or a personal perspective—consider in which ways teens can learn how to better use traditional categorization systems in conjunction with their use of tagging technologies.

Comparing Technologies

Contemplate the library catalog that includes both traditional search capabilities and tags. As mentioned above, a teen can search that catalog using the traditional or tag method. But if the teen searches using tags, what will the result be? Will he or she find the best information available on the topic? Not necessarily. Will the results be so personal in nature that they make no sense in the context of the teen's research needs? Possibly. Will he or she be assaulted by more results than it's possible to even think about? Perhaps.

If the answers to those questions are as suggested, then the integration of tags with traditional searching techniques could make the teen research process even more difficult than it already is. Yet the integration of tags into library catalogs is something that should take place. That means that a balance must be struck and an understanding of when to search by tags and when to search by traditional terminologies and structures needs to be a part of a teen's set of research skills.

The first step in reaching that balance is to help teens understand the global vs. personal nature of traditional and tag searching methods. A perfect example of that is a search for "me" in a library catalog (that integrates tags) and a site like Flickr. It's likely that in a library catalog a search for "me" within the traditional search fields—author, title, subject, description, and notes—will turn up items in which "me" is a part of the title of a specific item. However, if teens search for "me" as a tag in the library catalog, they will find lists of materials in which the tagger simply wanted to connect the material to his or her personal interest. In other words the results in the traditional form lead to materials in which me is actually a part of the material—the title. But, the results using tags is all about the tagger and not about the content of the item.

Of course, it's rare that a teenager would search using a term such as "me" except within a forced construct of a lesson on tags vs. traditional catalog searching. It would make more sense to explore real searches with teens on topics that are of personal or school-related interest. For example, maybe a teenager is researching a topic of personal interest— for example, manga. While a library catalog search for that topic might be helpful in finding general information, the teen might also be interested in personal responses to manga by peers. In that case the teen would want to search for manga-related tags in order to access first-person insights into the genre. The manga search—using terminology both global and personal—would give teens the opportunity to explore what the differences are in results and why those differences exist.

Making Meaning

Using tags as a part of the research process can help teens expand their understanding of the topic they are studying. In her article on tagging, Mary Ellen Bates discusses why researchers have discovered that tagging is not the most successful method to use when searching for information. Bates also notes that tags can suggest new ideas to a researcher around a particular topic. She writes, "And sometimes a tag isn't applied in a way that I would consider proper, but it could prompt me to wonder why that person tagged that item with that term. Is there an aspect of the idea that I missed?" (Bates 2006). In other words, tags help teens make meaning out of their research topic while traditional cataloging search strategies helps students find research to support (or bring into question) teen understandings.

Considering Tag Clouds

Looking at and creating tag clouds also helps teens become more proficient searchers. Online tools are available for making personal tag clouds. Teens might use TagCloud.com to collect information from sites on a topic of interest. TagCloud takes the topic resources a teen submits and pulls out key tags from those resources. It then places those tags in a tag cloud visual.

This could be useful to teens who are researching a particular topic as a way to get started on keywords and research questions. For example, a teen might need to think about terms to use when researching Apple Computer. The teen would find sites on Apple and MAC computers and enter the RSS feed URL (learn about RSS in chapter 3.) for those sites into TagCloud.com. TagCloud would gather data from those sites in order to pull out the tags on that topic and display the information in a cloud. The teen researcher would then look at the tags in the cloud, analyze them within the context of the particular research need, test them out in a library catalog or online search tool, and use the terms that are most interesting at the moment to develop or refine research questions about the topic. Figure 4.3 shows a tag cloud on the Apple/MAC topic that uses a variety of RSS feeds on MAC and Apple.

Figure 4.3 Apple/MAC Tag Cloud.

Looking at the cloud in figure 4.3, a teen should start to realize what the popular topics are for people interested in Apple products. The teen might start to ask questions about the history of iPods and Apple's growth in the MP3 player market. He or she might formulate questions about the Apple operating system and what its benefits are over Microsoft's. The teen might decide to create a comparison tag cloud for Windows to see what the similarities and differences are in people's interests related to that company and to Apple Computer. Starting the research with a tag cloud provides teens with a chance to think about where to go in the research process and to refine ideas based on popular terminology.

For example, often librarians and teachers ask students to come up with questions and a set of keywords to use when researching a particular topic. Imagine if a part of this process integrated the use of tag clouds. A student would create a cloud on a topic of interest, analyze the cloud contents to determine possible research subtopics, and come up with questions about the topics based on the contents of the tag cloud. This type of activity combines text and visuals to enhance the research process.

WHEN, WHERE, WHY

Tags might create chaos. But inside of that chaotic structure are incredible opportunities for teens to enhance their literacy skills, learn more about who they are and how they fit into the world, and understand the research process. As a blogger put it, "Folksonomies enhance exploration. Taxonomies enhance searching" (Gahran 2005). Teens need to be able to explore. They need to be able to make their own meaning out of content. But tagging doesn't have to be used or presented in a vacuum; teens can also learn how tagging supports personal and academic research needs and learn to make smart decisions related to those needs. Examples mentioned above should help you get started.

5

Reading and Writing in a Gamer's World

> Again, video-game stories are not better or worse than stories in books and movies. They offer different pleasures and frustrations. (Gee 2003, 83)

Until recently much of the adult discussion about video games centered on the violence embedded in some of the games teenagers play. Many adults think that gamers simply spend time playing in order to take part in a passive entertainment. What has not been realized, until relatively recently, is that game play is far from passive, and that game play actually can improve literacy and learning. (As suggested by the title of James Gee's 2003 book, *What Video Games Have to Teach Us About Literacy And Learning.*) Fortunately, many educators, sociologists, business experts, and others have started to delve into game play and the application gaming skills have in education, business, and even in life. In this chapter we'll examine some of the recent research on the topic, what researchers discovered about teens and their literacy practices as they relate to the world of gaming, and how these practices have an impact on libraries and classroom.

GAMING VOCABULARY

A short and selected list of gaming terminology.

Console—The hardware that runs video games. The console is often connected to a TV, monitor, or projection system.

Controller—Joystick, buttons, dance pad, and so on. The hardware that is used to control the action in the game.

MUDs (Multi-User Domains)—Games in which players join in a game online. These games usually include role playing, chat and/or instant messaging, and some sort of virtual world. MUDs are usually text driven.

MMPORG (Massive Multi-User Online Role Playing Game)—Games in which thousands of people play together online. These games integrate role playing, chat and/or instant messaging, virtual worlds, and more. MMPORGs use high levels of graphics in the play.

RPGs (Role-Playing Games)—Games in which players take on roles and play from the perspective of that role. Dungeons and Dragons is an RPG.

SIMs (Simulations)—Games in which a player simulates something, for example, building a park, a city, or a roller coaster.

It's All There

As the quote that opens this chapter suggests, video games often focus on a story; and it's that story in which the player becomes immersed. All the elements of traditional story are included—character, theme, plot, setting, motivation, beginning, middle, end, and so on. In video games, as in other visual media, the elements of story are played out primarily in images. Yet that doesn't mean that teens who play video games never connect to text. That notion is far from the truth. Teen gamers also read:

- Online guides and books about characters
- Histories of the setting, characters, and so on in which the game takes place
- How to improve game play
- Online discussions about the game
- Fiction that fans of the game write in order to extend the game-playing experience (usually called fan fiction)

If teen gamers are writing fanfiction, not only does game play incorporate reading, it also includes writing. Along with writing fan fiction, teens write

- Postings on discussion boards
- Character studies
- Messages in chat sessions with fellow fans
- Game-related poetry
- Enhancements and modifications to a game story

Good Learning from Good Games

… If our brain really desired to atrophy in front of mindless entertainment, then the story of the last thirty years of video games … would be a story of games that grew increasingly simple over time…. The games are growing more challenging because there's an economic incentive to make them more challenging—and that economic incentive exists because our brains like to be challenged." (Johnson 2005, 182)

The foundation of literacy is found in all video games teens play. Of course some games provide opportunities to take part in the full complement of reading and writing activities, while others are much more limited in those areas. In his article "Good Video Games and Good Learning," James Paul Gee discusses 16 game components that support learning (Gee 2005), including the following:

Identity

In many games players take on specific roles or characters in order to move around the game and achieve success. This means that teens who play games can try on new identities, problem-solve as someone other then the person they are at school and at home, and succeed as the character or role they take on in the game. The positive impact of game play on identity is explicitly demonstrated in the final episode of the television series *Freaks and Geeks*. In this episode, the main "freak," Daniel, ends up playing Dungeons and Dragons with the geeks, who are long-time players of the game. In previous episodes viewers watched Daniel struggle with his identity. On the outside he is extremely cool, but viewers know that on the inside he is filled with self-doubt. Daniel has never been a successful student. By the final episode of the series, his poor school experiences are having an adverse effect on his self-esteem. When Daniel wins the game of dungeons and dragons, the viewer can't help but cheer his success. The look of joy on Daniel's face because he has succeeded in something, and in something that the smart kids excel at, gives viewers real hope that it was just Daniel's first positive gaming experience, and that Daniel might be on the road to a higher sense of self.

As mentioned in previous chapters, teens' sense of identity is intricately intertwined with their literacy practices. Teen reading and writing is more meaningful when related to the search for personal identity. In game play, as teens are immersed in the character and role they are playing, they are gaining literacy skills while at the same time learning about themselves.

Interaction

Teens interact with games by getting feedback as a result of the decisions they make during game play. They also interact with other game players via online and face-to-face discussions about games, how to play them more successfully, and so on. Chapters 3 and 4 discussed in detail the positive aspects of teen use of communication tools in order to interact with peers and experts. The interaction in games has the same value for teen literacy development. The extra feature in game play is that teens not only interact with other players, but they also interact with the game through the feedback that's received. Game feedback comes at many points that involve text and visuals. For example:

- Losing the game
- Winning the game
- Running out of money to purchase needed supplies or equipment
- Teammates deciding to join another team
- The player's character getting lost in the world of the game

Teens need to digest the feedback they receive in order to move forward in the game. This digestion can take many forms including analyzing what leads to defeat or success, writing about the game play, or talking to others about the game play. Each of these activities integrates literacy practices that help teens develop reading, writing, and communication skills.

Production

Teens playing video games produce content. They do this by the choices they make in a game and as a result produce a game that is unique to their experience, meaning that no two games are ever exactly the same. They also produce by creating fan fiction, character studies, online discussions, and so on.

In the video game world, teens produce in another way as well, when they have a chance to create their own games using techniques and skills learned through play. Teens who produce games face many literacy challenges including making decisions about characters, writing character sketches, determining sequences of events, writing instructions on playing the game, and so on.

Risk Taking

Game play wouldn't be game play if no risk were involved. Teens who play games are given the chance to try things out in order to find out what "would happen if" within an environment in which adverse results do not cause havoc in the real world. Being able to take risks is an important component of life in the real world. In the game world teens can experiment safely. Daniel, from *Freaks and Geeks,* was able to try out behavior in Dungeons and Dragons that would not be accepted by his peers or adults in his day-to-day world. He experimented, saw what happened, and moved on.

Gee uses the phrase "pleasantly frustrating" as one of the qualities of good games. There is a direct relationship between risk taking and frustration. When one takes a risk it's possible to be frustrated by the outcomes of that risk. That's not a bad thing and actually can produce a greater desire to keep trying—as long as it's possible to keep trying.

Performance Before Competence

Gee writes, "Players can perform before they are competent, supported by the design of the game, the 'smart tools' that the game offers, and often, too, the support of other, more advanced players (in multi-player games, in chat rooms, or standing there in the living room) (Gee 2005, 37)." In other words, teens are given multiple opportunities to try things out in a game. They don't have to excel as players until they have had time to practice, understand, and learn. Isn't this really what the writing process is all about? Teens write, rewrite, edit, revise, and so on as a way to build competent writing skills.

A WORD ABOUT LINEAGE

Simply playing Lineage requires facility with text, particularly in negotiating private, public, and other chat channels through which text constantly streams in real time. Players determine roles in groups, recruit new pledge members, negotiate through conflicts (such as competitions over the rights to hunt in territories), establish norms for collaborative events (such as hunts and sieges), theorize game play dynamics (such as where are the best places to hunt), and debrief. Outside of the game world, they tell stories, post screen shots, write poetry, search databases, post hints and walkthroughs, and generally "cuss and discuss" all aspects of game play, from character class design and military formations to social gossip and related real-world history. (Squire and Steinkuehler 2005, 39)

Lineage URL: http://www.lineage.com/

MAKING THE SELL

It's important that we as educators understand what makes a good game. Instead of dismissing a game because it's violent or because it seems silly, we need to look more deeply into behavioral development and consider how the classroom and library can support this development through gaming. While it might seem obvious to you why and how game play supports literacy development, it's possible that selling gaming to colleagues, administrators, parents, and others could prove difficult. Therefore, you need to be able to articulate simply and clearly the positive benefits of gaming in a teen's life. This includes the specific literacy points that are mentioned above as well as a few other points that follow.

No Game Play is Entirely Passive

Think about a game of solitaire. While it might seem like a mindless affair of putting cards on top of each other based on number or color, in reality the solitaire player needs to think about several things in order to be successful. There is planning involved. The same goes for a game like Snood, in which players aim to empty the screen by matching Snoods of the same color. Snood takes planning. The player needs to pay attention to what's available next in order to make the best decision at the current moment. All games—from Monopoly to Runescape to Sims—take planning and decision making. Of course, there are levels of planning and decision making, but no game play is entirely passive.

Gamers Do Not Play (or Live) in a Vacuum

In some people's minds, the word gamer brings up a vision of a teenage boy dressed in black sitting in his room at the computer playing a game completely alone. That vision is basically untrue. While the teen (boy or girl) might be sitting in a room alone, in many instances while playing an online game the teen is far from alone in the world of that game. The game play might include others from around the world. Beyond that, the game play might include chat, discussion threads, blogs, and so on with other teens from around the world. The gamer/gaming community is huge, and teen gamers get feedback from, make friends with, and collaborate with many others. Naturally, this is a bidirectional experience, as teens not only get information from others but they also transmit information to others. A teen then has to filter the information in order to determine what is most relevant to success in the game.

The Gamer's World is Not an Entirely Evil World

Whiles some may agree that teens aren't playing in a vacuum and aren't entirely alone when gaming, there is some fear that the other gamers teens play and communicate with are not those that adults would like the teen to be in contact with. Of course, there are some gamers of whom teens should be careful. The same safety techniques that are used in chat, e-mail, and blogging should be used in the online gaming environment. Teens need to be smart about those they play with and what they let others know about themselves within the gaming environment. Games are not the evil; it's what people do with the games and in the game environment that is sometimes evil. But then, evil things are done in the real world as well.

FOCUS ON LITERACY

LIBRARY GAMING CASE STUDY

Recently gaming was integrated into two branches of the New York Public Library. In order to bring gaming into the branches, library programming staff decided to work with branch library teen advisory groups to find out what the teens wanted to have in the way of games at the library and to work with the teens to plan gaming programs and library services.

The teens in the branch libraries were excited by the prospect of bringing games into their library. They had many ideas of what hardware and software to purchase. Some of the teens read through gaming magazine ads and reviews in order to decide on titles to add to the collection.

As a part of this project two unexpected subprojects were initiated. First, teens at one library decided it was important to educate adults in their community about gaming and why games are an important part of teen life. In order to accomplish something like this teens need to plan how they are going to encourage adults to attend meetings and how they are going to present the games to adults.

The second unexpected development was the library's hiring of one of the teens who participated in the project. The idea is that this teen will travel to library branches to show his peers how to play games. (He is a longtime gamer and an excellent player of almost every game he tries.) This is something brand new for the teen and the library. Before being hired, the teen needed to talk with librarians about what he could accomplish at the various branches. He needed to write a biography that could be used in advertising and be placed in his personnel file. And he needed to write a description of what each library workshop would include. The print literacy skills of this teen were in full use throughout this process.

Gaming in libraries and classrooms is currently a source of much excitement and discussion. Articles are available in professional journals about the positive implications of gaming in the lives of children, teens, and adults. That's great. However, the resulting learning and program and service changes in schools and libraries have been slow in coming and superficial in impact. As you bring games and gaming into the work you do with teens, make sure that the integration goes beyond rote learning or simply making games available as a "perk." Make an effort to integrate games into the classroom and library in meaningful ways that effectively support teen literacy skills.

It's wonderful if your library or classroom has games available for teens to play. It would be even better if you considered the following example as a chance to integrate gaming fully into the library or classroom.

Workshop Gaming

Many adults participate in events that allow them to "workshop" a novel or screenplay. Gamers can also be given the opportunity to workshop what they create as a part of the gaming experience. A teen writers workshop in which participants have the chance to create characters and worlds, write about game play, or create a brand new game story is a logical literacy-based learning experience and extension of the game play. The workshop might include a game designer who would take teens through the process of creating a game story that integrates choice and serendipity. Teens would need to go through all the steps of the writing process in order to develop their character, game, or world and as a result expand, enhance, and improve their writing and reading skills.

Of course teens might also build the technological back end of a new game they develop. However, the first steps in creating that back end have to be writing the game outline, developing the characters that will be a part of the game, and so on. One can't play any game if someone hasn't first built the people and events for that game.

Go Beyond Availability

The *Freaks and Geeks* character, Daniel, never succeeded in school. Yet in his first time playing he succeeded in Dungeons and Dragons. What was the difference? For one thing, playing Dungeons and Dragons gave Daniel the chance to practice all of the things James Gee discusses—search for identity, take risks, produce, content and so on. He did that by becoming part of a different world and taking on a character role with which he could be entirely himself or not. (In other words, he did whatever was necessary in order to succeed in the game.)

In educational environments, students need opportunities to succeed in the same way using the same types of skills and interests. By deconstructing the gaming environment, you can find ways to integrate the positive aspects of gaming into your teaching routine. What would a unit or lesson look like if presented in the format of a role-playing game? (This is different than a Webquest where students take on roles.) If teens are studying the Middle Ages, would it be possible to create a game like Lineage as their learning framework? Could you create histories, guides, and character studies like those associated with World of Warcraft and Runescape? Is it possible to develop a simulation framework around the Middle Ages so that teens create their own medieval community? The answer to all of those questions is yes. It takes thought, planning, and change. But it can be done.

As a librarian, think beyond simply getting teens to come to the library to play games or setting up gaming parties. While teens play games in the library, they are certainly using literacy skills. But you can go beyond simply providing the play, to providing specific opportunities for mediated literacy growth. The workshop example above is one way to do this. So too is integrating gaming programs and services in the same way print materials are integrated into programs and services. That means:

- Giving teens opportunities to read and write reviews about games and gaming
- Inviting game developers to speak to teens just like authors are invited to speak to teens
- Creating electronic communication environments where teens can talk to each other about games and game play
- Creating a gamers' teen advisory group to allow teens to make suggestions and decisions about game collections and game programming
- Giving teens the chance to lead workshops for parents and teachers on gaming

The point is, that providing a place to play should be only one part of the literacy experience of teen gamers.

POPULAR ONLINE GAMES

Lineage
    http://www.lineage.com/
Runescape
    http://www.runescape.com/
Second Life
    http://www.secondlife.com/
World of Warcraft
    http://www.worldofwarcraft.com/

FAD OR NOT

You might think that all of the hoopla over gaming in education is simply a fad that will fade out in a year or two. That is possible. But, that isn't necessarily a good thing. The positive literacy implications of gaming for teens are vast. It would therefore be unfortunate if you missed this opportunity. In order to not miss it, you must take to heart the positive literacy implications of gaming for teens and, as mentioned above, find meaningful ways of integrating them into your classroom or library.

PART III

Libraries and Classrooms as Virtual Communities

A look at how libraries and classrooms can support social networks and online community building with technologies that support teen literacies

6

Technology + Literacy = Social Networking

Community—1.a. A group of people living in the same locality and under the same government. b. The district or locality in which such a group lives. 2. A group of people having common interests. 3.a. Similarity or identity. b. Sharing participation and fellowship. 4. Society as a whole; the public. (American Heritage 1993, 282)

In chapter 1 of this book, we focused on how people define literacy and how the definition of literacy has changed over the decades and even over the centuries. It's possible to say the same of the definition of community. In previous decades, community was narrowly defined as a group of people who live in close proximity to each other. However, with the innovation of participatory and interactive technologies, it's possible to expand the definition of community to a much broader framework. Currently the phrase "social networking" is used to describe the communities built via technologies that incorporate many of the tools discussed throughout this book. In this chapter, we'll look more closely at how literacy and technology can work together to enable you in building viable virtual social networks for and with teens.

DEFINING COMMUNITY

It's possible to break community into at least three different levels (as shown in figure 6.1). The smallest and perhaps most central level of community for a teenager is the immediate/extended family. Once a teen moves out beyond that level, the world opens up in a variety of ways. In the middle level are those people whom teens encounter (and events in which they participate) within their town and in the school they attend. These are the parts of a teen's world that center on regular face-to-face interaction with others within a fairly small geographic region. The school and the library are parts of this second level of community for a teen, and it's the programs and services these institutions provide that help teens become a part of the physical library and education communities.

The third level of community for a teen is the largest ring within figure 6.1. It is where teens encounter a potentially great number of others in the online world. These are the people teens play games with in MMO Gaming (Massive Multiplayer Online Gaming) environments and who read the fan fiction that teens write and post on the Web. Teens who produce podcasts and those who listen to teen podcasts are a part of this larger community. When libraries and schools provide teens with opportunities to expand whom they know and communicate with via

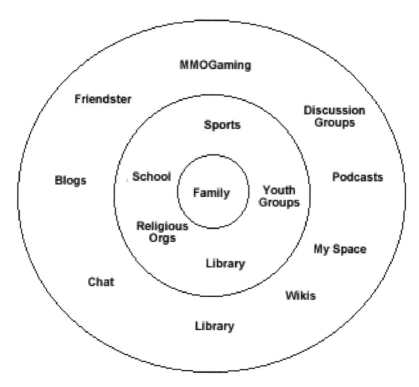

Figure 6.1. Levels of Teen Communities

blogs, chats, discussion boards, wikis, podcasts, and so on, they also become part of this realm. It's this larger realm of a teen's community that libraries and schools need to tap into in order to connect with and help teens with their expanded and new literacies.

MySpace

Any 16-year-old can tell you that logging on to MySpace.com is as vital to teen culture as showing your face at the right party. (Hempel and Buecke 2005, 9)

An example of a virtual community popular with teens is MySpace, where anyone who registers for the site can build a virtual space that may include a blog, a message board, photo albums, instant messaging, music, and more. A teen builds a house at MySpace, and others can visit that teen there. It's an example of a place where connections are made based on interests. For example, a MySpace teen might note that she likes the music of Death Cab for Cutie. Another teen can search MySpace for Death Cab for Cutie, find the teen that mentioned them at MySpace, and then send that teen a message. They start a conversation with others with the same musical taste and before too long a social network of Death Cab for Cutie fans from around the world is built, all via the MySpace Web interface.

Authors, librarians, and educators are now using MySpace as a way to build community with their readers and their users. You can visit *Gingerbread* author Rachel Cohn's MySpace space at http://www.myspace.com/rachel_cohn and learn quite a bit about the young adult fiction author. You find out what she likes to read, listen to, and view. You also have the chance to tell her what you think about the books she's written, find out what she's working on now, and see who her other friends are. Rachel Cohn's MySpace space is a perfect example of providing teens and authors with a way to connect with each other. Cohn says about her space, "It's a great way to meet your readers and get to know them" (Cohn 2006). It's also a great way for Cohn's fans to connect with each other. The 600+ friends of Rachel Cohn at MySpace represent a MySpace fan club, and it's a community of Rachel Cohn readers who get to talk about her books with her and each other at MySpace.

Teen users of the Hennepin County Library can connect with each other via that library's MySpace space available at http://www.myspace.com/hennepincountylibrary. In this space teens can send messages to the library and can also search the library catalog, find out about the library's programs and services, and read the library's MySpace blog. The library's use of MySpace is a perfect example of helping to build teen community using the tools and technologies with which teens are comfortable.

"MySpace's success stems from its focus on pop culture, as opposed to technology for its own sake" (Rosenbush 2005). In a MySpace space teens focus on what they are interested in—not what adults think they should be interested in. It's that personal connection to real life that makes the space meaningful and makes it work for the audience.

In order for teens to find and communicate with each other via MySpace they have to use literacy skills. Writing a message to the Death Cab for Cutie fan, reading the message from the Death Cab for Cutie fan, building a base of fans: All require reading and writing skills. As a social network, MySpace is a hotbed of and for literacy.

"The first social networking website was Classmates.com, which began in 1995. Other sites followed, including SixDegrees.com, which began in 1997. It was not until 2001 that websites using the Circle of Friends online social networks started appearing. This form of social networking, widely used in virtual communities, became particularly popular in 2003 and flourished with the advent of a website called Friendster. There are over 200 social networking sites, though Friendster is one of the most successful at using the Circle of Friends technique."

Source: Wikipedia. Available at http://en.wikipedia.org/wiki/Social_network. Entry updated June 12, 2006.

THE LIBRARY AND SCHOOL BUILD TEEN SOCIAL NETWORKS

The library and school can be hotbeds of literacy and social networking too. There are a few examples of libraries as teen virtual community builders (for example, a library MySpace space). But librarians and educators can also learn from the social networks created by other organizations in order to build virtual communities for teens. In the following section of this chapter we'll:

- Take a look at one library agency model and one nonlibrary model of teen social networking
- Consider how a library's integration of commenting features in the catalog can build teen community
- See how libraries and schools can combine virtual social networking with face-to-face social networking in order to give teens a variety of opportunities to connect with others

My Own Café

My Own Café is a Web site developed by the Southeast Massachusetts Regional Library System (SEMLS) as a way to provide teens with one-stop access to online resources. In the process of developing the site, SEMLS discovered another need of teens—beyond the need to have an easy way to access database articles: the need for a place where teens within southeastern Massachusetts could meet others from the area to talk about interests, needs, experiences, and so on. This building of local community happens at My Own Café via the discussion boards on topics of interest to local teens. There are discussion boards on local events, on politics, and on entertainment.

Figure 6.2. My Own Café

However, SEMLS was able to use technology to help build teen community in another way when planning the site. In order to get teen input, the library sponsored a series of chat sessions for the teen advisers who helped build content and look and feel. Teens from a variety of libraries in the area took part in the chat sessions and were able, in these chats, to find out what they had in common, what their differences were, and how to sell ideas to the adults who were ultimately responsible for building the site.

Via the chats, teens were asked to articulate their ideas about My Own Café. They had to express their ideas in a way that would make sense and would resonate with others in the room at the moment. Also, because the chat transcripts were read after the chats by planners and site designers, teens had to make sure, even when they used chat language, that they were able to make a point in a way that would be understood both during the chat session and afterwards.

During the chat sessions something else important happened—teens got to talk about online safety, what they knew about staying safe online, and what they thought SEMLS needed to do in order to keep teens at My Own Café safe. Communicating these ideas in a virtual space gave the teens, from a variety of towns, the chance to safely talk about the issues in an environment that was comfortable and welcoming. They could be somewhat anonymous while at the same time be a part of a community that was important to them.

My Own Café URL: http://www.myowncafe.org/

Friendster

Friendster preceded MySpace, and while there is much more talk today about MySpace, the capabilities of Friendster should not be ignored as they relate to literacy and building community: "It's important for me to choose friends that share my values, ideas, and goals in life because then we can talk about things and these discussions reinforce our choices and convictions. You could say that I want to look at my friends and see myself reflected in them, that my choices of friends define me" (Azmitia, Ittel, and Rachmacher 2005, 23). This quote from a teenager who took part in a study on the importance of friendships to an adolescent's sense of self gets to the heart of what makes the Friendster social networking model important.

After registering at Friendster, a person (from now on known as a friend) makes a list of likes including movies, TV, music, and so forth. Each like becomes a tag in that "friend's" profile. Once information is entered the friend can click on one of the tags to find others who listed the same like. (It's quite exciting to find a long list of others who like the same things, and somewhat deflating when no one has the same likes.)

It's possible to ask others to become a friend, and when the friend request is accepted that friend is listed on the original friend's profile page. Friends can communicate with each other via instant messages, e-mail, and discussion board–type postings. Friendster also keeps track of important events—for example, friends' birthdays—and Friendster sends reminders when an event is coming up and needs attention.

Having a Friendster profile without any friends listed can be troubling; imagine logging into the site and seeing "you have no friends" on the page. So, once registered for Friendster, finding others with like interests is definitely the thing to do. More friends means more popularity. Just like in the halls of high school, being popular at Friendster is important. But remember that since the world of Friendster is much larger than the world of a local high school, the chances of becoming popular are definitely greater.

Friendster URL: http://www.friendster.com/

Hennepin County Library Catalog

It's nothing new for a library catalog to be available on the Web. And it's not very new to have a graphical catalog that integrates book covers into the display of a particular title. What is new is the integration of reader comments into the display of book information. Amazon and other store sites have included customer comments for many years. But in the spring of 2006 the Hennepin County Library added commenting to their library catalog.

The commenting feature is very simple to use. Search for a title in the catalog. Click on the title on the results list. When in the title record click on the comment icon. There you can add a comment and read what others have written about the particular title.

It's pretty obvious that the commenting requires that teens use literacy skills in order to read and write comments on a specific item. But what might not be as obvious is the way that this feature allows libraries to build community around items owned by the library. Imagine that your library discovers that dozens of teens are commenting on a particular title in the catalog. If that's the case, then it's the perfect time to sponsor a face-to-face program on the theme of the item or the item itself. Why not bring teens together to talk about what they are interested in at that very moment?

Giving teens the chance to find others who have similar interests (through sites like MySpace, My Own Café, Friendster, and library catalog commenting features) helps guarantee that they are comfortable with who they are, which, as mentioned in previous chapters, is an important aspect of adolescent literacy. If a teen can locate others online with the same interests in music, movies, TV, and so on, then that teen knows that he or she is not alone. Geeks and cool kids alike find connections in the virtual world that help make them feel better about themselves and the world in which they live.

Hennepin County Library catalog URL: http://catalog.hclib.org/

The Perfect Library or Classroom Social Network

It doesn't exist, yet, but there is a perfect opportunity for you to build a social network that connects what your organization does well with what teenagers enjoy about technology. This network would incorporate technologies and ideas found in Friendster, 43 Things (discussed in chapter 4), and library catalog commenting features to build a community for teens that is both virtual and face-to-face. If you're a teacher, you'll want to collaborate with your school or local public librarian to do this.

What does it look like? A library gives teens who use a barcode number or other registration format the opportunity to register for, we'll call it, My Favorite Things. Registration requires entry of the teen's library card number, a username, and a password. Once registered, the teen can tag library materials and make lists of favorite and nonfavorite items owned by the library. Teens can also find others who have tagged items the same way (similar to Friendster) and can communicate with each other about likes and dislikes.

This part of My Favorite Things makes up the virtual social networking that teen's can take part in via the library's Web site. But you don't have to stop at the virtual network. Once teens find each other via

My Favorite Things, you can host meet-ups for teens who discovered like interests online. Each week, or month, your school or library can host meet-ups for all of those who like a particular type of music or band. You might invite My Favorite Things users to inform teachers or library staff of the meet-ups that should happen regularly. Ultimately, this allows teens to meet each other in a safe environment. And since a library barcode number is used at the time of registration for My Favorite Things, you should have some sense of security knowing that people who attend the meet-ups are a part of your library's user database.

BUILDING SOCIAL NETWORKS AT YOUR LIBRARY OR IN YOUR CLASSROOM

It's clear that there are some who have discovered ways to help teens use new technologies and new literacies to build social networks both small and large. But making it happen isn't always easy. One of the first requirements is educating administrators and other members of your local community—principals, school boards, trustees, parents, co-workers, and so on—about why it is important to help teens expand their literacies and their community via technology.

How can it be done? There are a variety of ways to accomplish this, including workshops, meetings, and informal education. A starting place is to be able to articulate why print technology literacy and virtual social networking are important for teens. The following talking points are provided as a first step in articulating ideas related to these topics to administrators, co-workers, and others.

Talking Points
Digital Natives/Digital Immigrants

Any 13-year-old in the year 2006 lives in a world that has included technology for his or her entire life. The first home computer game, Pong, was released 21 years before the teenager was born. These are teens who have used technology in all aspects of their lives including learning, playing, and socializing. Technology is native, and natural, to them.

Digital immigrants were not born into a technology-based world and as a result need to accept the fact that the world they were used to, and felt comfortable in, is different—some might say very different—from the one a digital native knows and understands.

While digital immigrants might feel uncomfortable multitasking, playing games as a way of learning and connecting with others, using

Web sites to build relationships, and so on, that is not the case for many digital natives. It's the unfamiliarity of the methods that makes digital immigrants uncomfortable. But, what's unfamiliar to an older generation is what's familiar to a younger one. And that familiarity helps build interest and excitement and also supports learning and literacy.

Brains Change

It's true—brains change based on what they are asked to do. "Neuroplasticity is the ability of the brain to physically change in response to stimulus and activity" (Wikipedia 2005). Research shows that through hard work on the part of students and teachers, and through intense study, physical changes in the brain occur (Roylance 2000). Think about the intensity with which teenagers participate in online activities. This is no doubt having an impact on the way that teen brains work. Those working with teens—teachers, librarians, and others—must therefore consider the impact of these changes on the way teenagers live, learn, play, and socialize. A digital immigrant's brain could very well be different than that of a digital native. The way a digital native learns is therefore different from the way a digital immigrant learns.

Learning Happens

Just because it is something a teen wants to do with her time doesn't mean that it's bad for her. "Today's learners are *different*. 'Every time I go to school I have to power down,' complains a high-school student. Is it that Digital Natives *can't* pay attention, or that they *choose not to?* Often from the Natives' point of view their Digital Immigrant instructors make their education *not worth* paying attention to compared to everything else they experience—and then they blame them for not paying attention!" (Prensky 2001, 3). Teenagers who are digital natives learn by participating in social networks because simply being in that network requires that they read and write and communicate in a way that makes sense to them and is exciting.

Remember, in order to use technologies successfully, teens need to have reading and writing skills. While they might communicate with others using a language that is unfamiliar to digital immigrants, that language makes complete sense to those with whom the teen is communicating. That means communication does indeed happen.

Building Self-Esteem

Adolescents need to know they are not alone. Sometimes in school and at home, it's easy to feel alone. But with virtual social networks it's often easier to find others who have similar experiences and communicate with them. That communication improves literacy because teens need to help others understand what they are thinking and show where commonalities, and differences, exist. Once teens find they are not alone in their problems, likes, and dislikes they usually become more secure in who they are.

Safety Is Possible

It can't be ignored. Safety is something that needs consideration when developing social networks. It doesn't matter what the age group is for the social networks (children, teens, or adults), there are possible dangers. However, just because something has the potential for danger doesn't mean that it should be ignored. Instead, the dangers need to be addressed and prevented or minimized.

To start, it's important to look at the pros and cons of the network under development. Why build the network? Because it will give teens the chance to meet others with like interests and it gives librarians and teachers the opportunity to connect teens to resources and peers in a safe environment. How do you guarantee teen safety in a virtual network environment? You specifically lay down ground rules for behavior in the virtual space. You define who can and cannot register for using the space. You talk to a lawyer and public safety official about problems that might arise and how to deal with those problems. Ultimately, it is impossible to guarantee a teen's safety in the social network the school or library might develop. However, it's also impossible to guarantee a teen's safety in the physical school or library space. But if adults work with teens to show them how to be safe in virtual environments and help them understand how to be safe in these environments, then their chances of staying safe online and off increase tremendously.

DOPA (DELETING ONLINE PREDATORS ACT)

In spring 2006 the U.S. Congress began to consider legislation that would prohibit a minor's ability to access social networking sites in schools and libraries. The Deleting Online Predators Act is seen by Congress as an extension of the Children's Internet Protection Act (CIPA). "DOPA would add an additional requirement. It says that libraries, elementary and secondary schools must prohibit 'access to a commercial social-networking Web site or chat room through which minors' may access sexual material or be 'subject to' sexual advances. Those may be made available to an adult or a minor with adult supervision 'for educational purposes'" (McCullagh 2005). [As of this writing, the bill is pending legislation.]

You can read more about DOPA at the American Library Association Washington Office http://www.ala.org/ala/washoff/washnews/2006ndx/ 053may12.htm.

No Dust

In the spring of 2005 when introducing speakers at a session of the New Jersey Library Association Annual Conference, Cathy Delneo stated, "Libraries have to do this or else they will be dust" (Delneo 2005). In her introduction Delneo was referring to the importance of integrating gaming and games into library programs and services for teens. Now it's time to extend that concept to say that schools and libraries need to build virtual communities for teens, or else they will be dust.

Digital natives are already using technology to build social networks. It's up to you to determine the best way to integrate those networks into the programs and services you provide.

- You can do it by looking at and using MySpace, Friendster, My Own Café, and the various technologies discussed in this and previous chapters of this book.
- You can do it by keeping up with the technologies teens use.
- You can do it by knowing when technology of teen interest has gone from cool to passé.
- You can do it by knowing why teens use these technologies and how the technologies support teen print literacy development.
- You can do it by not making assumptions.
- You can do it if you believe you can!

It might be difficult for digital immigrants to make it happen. But by their very nature schools and libraries build community, and a school or library online social network will help teens and help keep education, literacy, and learning alive.

7

A World of Ideas

My head often spins with new ideas and information. I read something, hear something, watch something and I say to myself, "Oh my gosh, I can do this, this, this, and this." I then try to determine what's the best idea to start with and what steps to take in order to begin.

In this book's previous chapters many ideas for integrating technology into the classroom or library are mentioned. Some ideas might have jumped out at you as something you want to start immediately. Some might not seem appropriate at the moment but you thought, "maybe, someday." You might want to mix and match some ideas. Before introducing other ideas you might need to provide some education to your community, colleagues, and administrators.

The following provides an overview of the technology integration ideas mentioned throughout this book.

INTEGRATING INSTANT AND TEXT MESSAGING—ROUND-UP, CHAPTER 2

Chat and text messaging are technologies that continue to gain in popularity. More and more teens remind me that if I want to connect with them it should be through chat and text messaging. They say that if I send an e-mail I need to IM too in order to let them know an e-mail is waiting. As mentioned in chapter 2, there are many text-based literacy skills used in both chat and IM. In the library and classroom you can support the use of these technologies in the following ways:

- Readers' Advisory

  Set up an IM service in which teens chat with you about what to read next. Or they can tell you about what you should make sure to put on your reading list. This can be a teen-managed service in which teens in the school or library are responsible for managing the service at specific times during the day or night.

- Gift-Giving Advice

  Use IM as a way to talk with teens about what to buy as gifts for friends and family members. Chat about interests and then suggest books, movies, music, DVDs, games, etc. This is another service that can be teen managed. Ask teens to create lists of suggestions that they can use as they chat with peers about gift-giving options.

- Study Groups

  Host regular study groups in which teens meet together to work on homework and socialize all at the same time. Study groups would be made up of peers or teens who tutor and support younger students. Don't forget that IM transcripts of study sessions give teachers, librarians, and parents the chance to support teens and younger students in their homework needs.

- New Book Notifications

  Use text messaging to alert teens of new materials in which they might be interested. Let teens know when a new book by a favorite author is available. Let them know when the newest title in a favorite genre comes into the library. Or let them know when a book they need for their homework is available for check-out or use in the library or classroom.

- Homework Reminders

  Don't let teens forget when that homework assignment is due. Send regular reminders of what they need to have ready for class the next day or the next week. Consider setting up a text messaging system in which teens can text the school and find out what's next on their homework list by keying in their name, grade, and teacher.

INTEGRATING BLOGS, WIKIS, AND PODCASTS—ROUND-UP, CHAPTER 3

Blogs might seem like an obvious opportunity for integrating text-based literacy skills into the library or classroom. Wikis, since they are primarily text driven might, seem pretty obvious as a literacy tool as well. But maybe you hadn't thought about the opportunities that podcasts provide for supporting print literacies. The ideas below focus on how each of these technologies can be used in classrooms and libraries in order to help teens read and write successfully.

- Blogs as a Publishing Platform

  A classroom or student blog becomes the publishing platform for teen-written work. As the last step in the writing process, a student publishes content to the blog and provides opportunities for parents, classmates, teachers, and librarians to read what that student learned and understands.

- Blog Bibliography

  A blog can be a place where students link to Web sites that support areas of study and a place to take notes the on reading, viewing, and listening that is a part of research and study.

- Reaction Blogging

  Teens read, view, hear, and say meaningful and not so meaningful things all the time. A library or classroom blog is a perfect platform for teens to react to what is going on around them. Peers and classmates comment on the reaction blog as a way to expand ideas and develop understanding of something going on in the teen's day-to-day world.

- News Blog

  Instead of a school newspaper or library newsletter, a news blog is a good way to give teens the chance to write about current local, national, and international events. Writing a news blog is a little different than writing a personal blog as teens would be expected to write as a journalist instead of as a diarist.

- Revision Wiki

  The history screen of a wiki is a great way to keep track of changes in a piece of writing. Teens can use a wiki to write drafts and revise work and use the history portion of their wiki to see how their work changed over time.

- Wiki Class/Meeting Notes

  Teens can use a wiki as a way to take notes in class or on a teen advisory group or other meeting. One teen starts the day's wiki notes and peers add to it from their own memory or written notes of what happened during a class session or meeting. Other teens can add to or change the notes. These group notes are a good way to keep track of content, learning, and group and individual responsibilities.

- Research Wiki

  As an individual teen or group of teens performs research on a topic, a wiki is a great place to keep track of information uncovered, bibliographic content, citations, and so on.

- What I Like About ... Wiki

  Teens might create a wiki on a topic of interest as a way to gather together information from lots of different people and resources. For example, a teen might start a wiki on heavy metal music. He or she would add information on bands, styles, and so on. Then other teens could add to the wiki information on the topic. Eventually, the wiki becomes a complete and up-to-date encyclopedia on heavy metal music.

- Thumbs Up/Down Podcast

  Creating podcast reviews of books, movies, music, Web sites, and so forth, is one way that audio can be integrated into the classroom or library. Teens who create the review casts might write scripts or outlines, select music to edit into the files, and investigate the best way to distribute the files via RSS.

- This Week in ... Podcast

  Weekly podcasts of content discussed in class are a great way for teens to explain concepts and cement learning. Groups of students might be responsible for the casts from week to week. Those creating the podcast would be responsible for reviewing academic content and those listening would have a second opportunity to gain understanding.

- Great Events Podcasts

  Have teens record events in the school or library. As a part of the recording process, teens would be responsible for gathering permission from speakers/presenters. They would be responsible for setting up the recording, adding introductory and closing information and music, and editing the content before distribution to subscribers/listeners.

INTEGRATING TAGGING—ROUND-UP, CHAPTER 4

Tagging provides teens with opportunities to describe content in terms that are meaningful to them. Librarians and teachers can help teens understand how to determine the best words to use in tag descriptions, when tagging is a useful online tool, and how to use tagging of information in order to organize and research topics of interest.

- What's Good? What's Not?

  Give teens the chance to use tags to describe the positive and negative qualities of particular areas of content. They might come up with one-word terms to describe the attributes of a good video game, movie, book, photo, and so on. They would then use those terms to describe various pieces of content in the library catalog or databases (if tagging is available), a photo-sharing Web site like Flickr, and so on.

- My Life When I …

  Teens might use tagging to describe experiences they will have or that they have had recently. Perhaps on a blog or Web site like 43 Things teens use one-word descriptors to tell others about their lives. For example, a blog entry about a family vacation might include terms such as California, car, long, hot, funny, boring, cool, San Francisco, or food.

- Clouds of Meaning

  Use tag clouds as a way for teens to chart events and interests over a specific period of time. For example, have teens look at the "Hot tags this hour" at Technorati over a predefined period of time. Ask them to chart the similarities and differences in taggers' interests and consider what events in the world at large have an impact on what people are writing about and reading.

- Search Experts

  Use tags as a way to teach teens about keyword searching and how to determine the best search terms to find information on a particular topic. Ask teens to compare the terms they might use to describe content with the terms they find work successfully when searching a library catalog or database.

INTEGRATING GAMING—ROUND-UP, CHAPTER 5

Gaming presents a host of opportunities for supporting text-based literacies in the classroom or library. Teens talking about gaming, teaching gaming, and learning about games and game play—all of these present literacy opportunities. Consider the following as you think about integrating gaming into your classroom or library:

- Games—By Teens for Adults

  Sponsor an event in which teens host a gaming open house. Teen hosts talk to adults about why they like to play games and how to play the games. Teens get to decide what games to showcase, how to advertise, and how to make the event a success.

- Teen Game Leaders

  Teens host gaming events for their peers or younger children in the classroom or library. They set up game stations and then help the others play the games successfully.

- Game Selectors

  Teens read reviews, play games, and select what the library should purchase. They can also write reviews for the library Web site or print publications.

- Expert Gamers

  Invite expert game players to your classroom or library to help teens learn tips and tricks in order to become experts themselves.

- Gamers Podcast

  Have teams of teens produce a weekly podcast. The cast might include tips and tricks on how to play specific games and reviews of recently released games. Teens who create the podcast might write outlines and scripts, select music, and edit the audio files.

- Dance Dance Classroom or Library

  Invite a choreographer, dance teacher, or dancer to the library to teach teens how to choreograph Dance Dance Revolution (DDR) routines.

- Workshop Gaming

  Have teens go through the entire process of creating a game from developing the story line, plot, characters, themes, and so forth. Invite game creators to help the teens turn their ideas into an actual game.

SOCIAL NETWORKING—ROUND-UP, CHAPTER 6

As teens move towards adulthood they need to figure out who they are. One of the ways they do this is by finding out how to articulate ideas and finding others that have similar ideas and interests. Now technology can help teens in this area of identity building. For example:

- I Have This to Say About …

  Investigate adding commenting technologies into the features of the library catalog and/or databases. Giving teens the chance to comment on what they read, view, or hear helps guarantee that they use text-based literacies on a regular basis.

- Library Space

  Teens want to talk to each other about what they like and don't like. They want to find others with the same or similar interests. Use MySpace or your own library Web site to give teens the chance to connect with peers as they write about their interests and read about the interests of others.

- My Favorite Things

  Create a Web space for teens in which they get to tag materials, ideas, images, and so forth in ways that help them to define their likes and dislikes. Then use what is included in the My Favorite Things space as a way to bring teens into the library for programs that reflect interests and needs noted within the My Favorite Things space.

MAKING IT WORK

Remember, you don't have to do everything right away. Start by thinking about your community, what you can actually achieve, and how you can use the first projects that you take on as a way to educate colleagues, administrators, and the community as a whole about the positive aspects of technology on teen text-based literacy skills. Use your successes to expand your capabilities.

It's likely that once you start thinking about the ways teens use technology and begin providing instruction and services that support that use, new ideas will come to mind on a regular basis. Don't forget to talk to teens about your ideas and about their use of technology and how it helps them to be better readers and writers. Who knows, maybe you will start a blog, a wiki, or another resource to keep track of what you are thinking and doing, your successes and challenges, and what teens have to say about technology's impact on their reading and writing lives.

APPENDIX A

Web-Based Content Creation Tools

BLOGS

The following is a short selected list of Web-based tools that can be used for setting up and maintaining a blog. They do not require any knowledge of HTML coding in order to get started.

Blogger
http://www.blogger.com

Live Journal
http://www.livejournal.com/

Type Pad
http://www.typepad.com/

Xanga
http://www.xanga.com/

If you or a colleague have the ability to download, install, or configure software on a server the following highly customizable software is available.

Movable Type
http://www.sixapart.com/movabletype/

Word Press
http://wordpress.org/

WIKIS

The following is a short selected list of Web-based tools to use to set up a wiki. These tools provide what's needed to get started in using wikis with teens.

JotSpot
http://www.jotspot.com/

PB Wiki
http://www.pbwiki.com

Wiki Spaces
http://www.wikispaces.com/

If you are able to download, install, and configure software on a server MediaWiki, you might want to try out http://www.mediawiki.org/wiki/MediaWiki (the highly customizable software behind Wikipedia).

PODCASTS/VODCASTS

There are tools on the Web that can be used to create and/or host podcasts. The following is a short selected list of some of those that are available.

AudioBlogger
http://www.audioblogger.com/

Odeo
http://www.odeo.com/

PodServe
http://pod-serve.com/

Appendix B

Finding and Catching Blogs and Podcasts

Finding Blogs

The following is a list of tools you can use to find blogs on a host of topics.

Google Blog Search
http://blogsearch.google.com/

Technorati
http://www.technorati.com/

Technorati searches blogs that are registered at the site. Someone who registers at Technorati can tag their blog with specific keywords and subject headings.

Yahoo! News Search
http://news.search.yahoo.com/

Yahoo's news search covers blogs as well as traditional news resources.

Finding Podcasts/Vodcasts

The following is a list of tools you can use to locate and subscribe to podcasts and vodcasts.

iTunes
http://www.itunes.com/

Before using iTunes you need to download and install the software on your computer. Once that's done you can search out podcasts and vodcasts in the iTunes Music Store.

Odeo
http://www.odeo.com/

With Odeo you search out podcasts and listen to them via the Web-based subscription and podcatching tool.

Podcast Alley
http://www.podcastalley.com/

At Podcast Alley you can find podcasts and vote for your favorite one.

Yahoo! Podcasts
http://podcasts.yahoo.com/

The Yahoo! podcast directory allows you to search out podcasts, subscribe to podcasts, and listen to podcasts.

SUBSCRIBING WITH RSS READERS AND PODCATCHERS

Bloglines
http://www.bloglines.com

Bloglines is a Web-based RSS reader. Once you set up an account you can subscribe to feeds in which you are interested.

iTunes
http://www.itunes.com/
Once you download iTunes on your computer you can use it as a podcatcher. Use the iTunes Music Store to find podcasts in which you are interested and then subscribe to them in iTunes.

NetNewsWire
http://www.newsgator.com/NGOLProduct.aspx?ProdID = NetNewsWire

This is MAC software you download and install on your computer. Once you do so you can subscribe to RSS feeds and customize the frequency with which the software goes out and looks for new information from the sites to which you subscribe.

NewsCrawler
http://www.newzcrawler.com/

A popular Windows-based program that collects RSS feeds and podcasts. This software is highly customizable and allows you to create settings for each feed individually.

Odeo
http://www.odeo.com/

The Odeo site functions as both a directory of podcasts and as a podcatcher. Subscribe to podcasts on Odeo and listen to them on the site too.

APPENDIX C

All About Technology

Check out the following resources—books, blogs, Web sites, and podcasts—in order to keep up with technology:

- That's new and emerging
- That teens use
- Suitable for schools and libraries.

Not all of the resources listed focus specifically on teens or on the educational applications of technology; however, it's often useful to consider what's happening in the consumer or technical worlds and the implications trends in other fields have for schools and libraries.

Don't forget that many of the resources allow you to subscribe to an RSS feed or a podcast.

Barron, Ann E., Karen S. Ivers, Nick Lilavois, and Julie A. Wells. (2006). *Technologies for Education: A Practical Guide,* Fifth Edition. Westport, CT: Libraries Unlimited.

The latest edition of this book includes information on using audio and video technology in classrooms and libraries.

Educause

http://www.educause.edu/

Read and view presentations and reports that focus on how educators are using and thinking about using technology in the classroom and library.

Engadget

http://www.engadget.com/

Find out what new gadgets have just been released or are about to be released. Both an Engadget blog and a podcast are available.

Farmer, Lesley S. J. (2005). *Digital Inclusion: Teens and Your Library*. Westport, CT: Libraries Unlimited.
Successfully covers why and how to support the technology use of teens who are nontraditional library users.

Harris, Frances Jacobson. (2005). *I Found It On the Internet: Coming of Age Online*. Chicago: ALA.
Provides specific examples and techniques for helping teens to use technology safely and ethically.

Pew Internet & American Life Project http://www.pewinternet.org/
The Pew Internet & American Life Project regularly publishes reports that explain and explore how Americans do and do not use technology. Several of their reports focus on teen use of technology in and out of school.

Richardson, Will. (2006). *Blogs, Wikis, Podcasts, and Other Powerful Web Tools for Classrooms*. Thousand Oaks, CA: Corwin Press.
A resource for gaining ideas on using Web-based collaborative reading and writing tools in the classroom.

RSS4Lib
http://blogs.fletcher.tufts.edu/rss4lib/
Find out how libraries are using RSS in this blog.

TechCrunch
http://www.techcrunch.com/
This blog is updated regularly with news about new tools and applications being developed for or available on the Web.

TWiT.tv
http://www.twit.tv/
TWiT.tv is the umbrella site for several technology podcasts including This Week in Tech (TWiT) and Inside the Net. Each of these is a great resource for finding out the latest news in technology and the latest trends in Web development.

Weblogg-ed
http://www.weblogg-ed.com/
Technology educator Will Richardson's blog brings technology news to educators in a thought-provoking way.

Wired News
http://www.wired.com/
Reading Wired News is a great way to keep up with the technology trends, successes, and flops.

Ypulse
http://ypulse.com/
A blog all about teen media—what's out there and how it is used.

References

The American Heritage College Dictionary (3rd ed.). (1993). Boston: Houghton Mifflin, 182.

Anderson, Larry S. (2005). Podcasting: Transforming Middle Schoolers into Middle Scholars. *T.H.E. Journal, 33*(5), 42–43.

Azmitia, Margarita, Angela Ittel, and Kimberley Radmacher. (2005). Narratives of Friendship and Self in Adolescence. *New Directions for Child and Adolescent Development, 107,* 23–39.

Bates, Mary Ellen. (2006, January/February). Tag—You're It. *Online, 30*(1), 64.

Blood, Rebecca. (2000). Weblogs: A History and Perspective. *Rebecca's Pocket.* Available at http://www.rebeccablood.net/essays/weblog_history.html#content.

Bush School Podcasts. (2005). Seattle, Washington. Available at https://www.bush.edu/home/news-detail.asp?pageaction=ViewSinglePublic&LinkID=859&ModuleID=42.

Campbell, Gardner. (2005). Something in the Air: Podcasting in Education. *Educause, 40*(6), 32–46.

Charlotte. (2005). *Sunday Morning Blog.* Available at http://www.livejournal.com/users/sunday__m0rning/112912.html#cutid1.

Cohn, Rachel. (2006, May). Personal conversation.

Delneo, Cathy. (2005, April 12). Introduction for Games @ Your Library. New Jersey Library Association Annual Conference, Long Branch, New Jersey.

Fabos, Cynthia, and Bettina Lewis. (2005) Instant Messaging, Literacies, and Social Identities. *Reading Research Quarterly, 40*(4), 470–501.

Flanagan, Brian, and Brendan Calandra. (2005). Podcasting in the Classroom. *Learning and Leading With Technology, 33*(3), 20–25.

Gahran, Amy. (2005). Strengths and Weaknesses of Metadata Schemes. *Contentious*. Available at http://blog.contentious.com/archives/2005/03/23/strengths-and-weaknesses-of-metadata-schemes.

Gee, James Paul. (2003). *What Video Games Have to Teach Us About Literacy and Learning*. New York: Palgrave Macmillan, 83.

Gee, James Paul. (2005). Good Video Games and Good Learning. *Phi Kappa Phi Forum, 85*(2), 33–37.

Gordon, Edward E., and Elaine H. Gordon. (2003). Literacy: A Historical Perspective. *Principal Leadership, 3*, 16–21.

Hempel, Jessi, and Dan Beucke. (2005, November 7). My Space Keeps Getting Bigger. *Business Week*, 9.

Houghton, Sarah. (2005, July/August). Instant Messaging: Quick and Dirty Reference for Teens and Others. *Public Libraries, 40*(44), 192–193.

Irving, Baily, Niall Janney, Molly Jordan, Annie Kass, Lucas Mayer, and Allison Rittershaus. (2004). Dear Bob Kerrey: Six Middleschoolers Tell How They Became Writers. *New England Reading Association Journal, 40*(1), 18–22.

Johnson, Steven. (2005). *Everything Bad Is Good for You*. New York: Riverhead Books, xiv, 183, 182.

Lenhart, Amanda, Mary Madden, and Paul Hitlin. (2005). "Teens and Technology: Youth are Leading the Transition to a Fully Wired Mobile Nation." Washington, DC: Pew Internet & American Life Project, p ii. Available at http://www.pewinternet.org/pdfs/PIP_Teens_Tech_July2005web.pdf.

Maney, Kevin. (2005, July 28). Sure in Text Messaging Makes Cell Operators 9. *USA Today*, 1b.

McCarroll, Christina. (2005, March 11).Teens Ready to Prove Text-Messaging Skills Can Score SAT Points. *Christian Science Monitor, 97*(74), 1.

McCullagh, Declan. Congress Targets Social Network Sites. C|Net News.com. Available at http://news.com.com/2100–1028_3–6071040.html.

Moore, David W., Thomas W. Bean, Deanna Birdyshaw, and James A. Rycik. (2000). Adolescent Literacy: A Position Statement. Available at http://www.reading.org/downloads/positions/ps1036_adolescent.pdf.

Nick W. (2005, January 25). Tags & Folksonomies—What Are They, and Why Should You Care? *Threadwatch*. Available at http://www.threadwatch.org/node/1206.

Osborne, Brian. (2005, May 27). Text Messaging Record Broken by American Idol Campaign. Geek.com PDA Geek. Available at http://www.geek.com/news/geeknews/2005May/bpd20050527030668.htm.

Pinker, Steven. (2000). *The Language Instinct*. New York: Harper Perennial, 262.

Prensky, Marc. (2001, October). Digital Natives Digital Immigrants. *On the Horizon*. NCB University Press, *9*(5).

Richardson, Will. (2005). What's a Wiki? A Powerful Collaborative Tool for Teaching and Learning That's What. *Multimedia and Internet @ School, 12*(6), 17–20.

Rosenbush, Steve. (2005, November 15). Users Crowd into MySpace. *Business Week Online.*

Rosenfeld, Louis. (2005). Folksonomies? How about Metadata Ecologies? Louis Rosenfeld.com. Available at http://louisrosenfeld.com/home/bloug_archive/000330.html.

Roylance, Frank D. (2000, May 27). Intensive Teaching Changes Brain Gains in Reading Last After Instruction Period, Study Finds. *Baltimore Sun.*

Seelye, Katherine. (2005, November 11). A Little Sleuthing Unmasks Writer of Wikipedia Prank. *New York Times,* A11.

Squire, Kurt, and Constance Steinkuehler. (2005). Meet the Gamers. *Library Journal, 130*(7), 38–41.

Sterling, Bruce. (2005). Order Out of Chaos. *Wired.* 13:04. Available at http://www.wired.com/wired/archive/13.04/view.html?pg=4.

Terdiman, Daniel. (2005). Adam Curry Gets Podbusted. News Blog C|Net News.com. Available at http://news.com.com/2061–10802_3–5980758.html.

Thompson, Robin C. (2004). "Me and Fiction Don't Get Along: New Times Literacy Strategies. Used by Early Adolescent Emerging Readers." PhD diss., University of South Florida.

Walker, Jill. (2005) Weblogs: Learning in Public. *On the Horizon 113*(2), 112–118.

Wikipedia. (2006). Neuroplasticity. Available at http://en.wikipedia.org/wiki/Neuroplasticity.

Williams, Bronwyn T. (2005/2006). Home and Away: The Tensions of Adolescent Community, Literacy and Identity. *Journal of Adolescent and Adult Literacy.* 49(4), 342–347.

Willis, Arlette. (1997). Focus on Research: Historical Considerations. *Language Arts, 74*(5), 387–397.

Index

Anderson, Larry S., 40
AOL, 20
AOL Messenger, 15
Author blogs, 32
Azmitia, Margarita, 76

Bates, Mary Ellen, 66
Blog, definition of, 27
Blood, Rebecca, 30
Buecke, Dan, 73
Bush School podcast, 44
Butler, Martina, 40,
   43, 45

Calandra, Brendan, 42
Campbell, Gardner, 42
Campfire, 21
Children's Internet Protection
   Act, 81
CIPA. *See* Children's Internet
   Protection Act
Classmates.com, 74
Cohn, Rachel, 73

Community, virtual, 35, 36, 37,
   63, 64, 66, 69, 71, 72, 73, 74,
   75, 76, 78, 79, 82
Curry, Adam, 36, 37

Daily Source Code, 37
Dance Dance Revolution, 50
DDR. *See* Dance Dance
   Revolution
Deleting Online Predators Act, 81
Delneo, Cathy, 82
Digital immigrants, 79, 80, 82
Digital natives, 79, 80, 82
DOPA. *See* Deleting Online
   Predators Act

East Oakland Community
   School podcast, 44
EmoGirlTalk, 40, 43

Fabos, Cynthia, 13, 14, 16, 17
Flanagan, Brian, 42
43 Things, 50, 52, 57

Freaks and Geeks, 59, 61, 66
Friendster, 74, 76, 77, 78, 82

Gahran, Amy, 56
Games, 50, 57, 58, 59, 60, 61, 62, 63, 64, 66, 72, 79, 82, 84, 87, 88
Gaming, vocabulary, 57
Gee, James, 57, 59, 61, 66
Google, 17, 22, 23, 26, 40, 43, 93
Gordon, Edward and Elaine, 3

Hempel, Jessi, 73
Hennepin County Library, 73, 77
Hitlin, Paul, 14, 18

Immigrants, 79, 80, 82
IMR. See Instant messaging
Instant messaging: definition of, 14; reference service, 20
Ittel, Angela, 76

Johnson, Steven, 4, 5, 59

Lenhart, Amanda, 14, 18
Lewis, Bettina, 13, 14, 16, 17
Library blogs, 32
Library podcasts, 41
Lineage, 61, 62, 66
Literacy: definition of, 4; history of, 5; and identity, 9; research, 8

Madden, Mary, 14, 18
Massive Multiplayer Online Gaming, 72
McCarroll, Christina, 14, 23
MMPORG. See Massive Multiplayer Online Gaming
MSN Messenger, 15

Natives, 79, 80, 82
Neuroplasticity, 80

Online games, 50, 57, 58, 59, 60, 61, 62, 63, 64, 66, 72, 79, 82, 84, 87, 88

Pew Internet in American Life Project, 15, 16, 18
Podcasting, definition of, 39
Podcatcher, definition of, 42
Pod Princess, 40, 43
Prensky, Mark, 90

Rachmacher, Kimberly, 76
Really Simple Syndication, 25
Rebecca's Pocket, 30
Richardson, Will, 35
Rich Site Survey, 25
Rosenbush, Steve, 74,
Rosenfeld, Louis, 52, 53
Roylance, Frank, 90
RSS. See Really Simple Syndication; Richardson, Will; Rich Site Survey

Safety, 29, 30, 63, 76, 81
Seigenthaler, John, 35, 36
SEMLS. See Southeast Massachusetts Library System
Short message system, 17
Skype, 15
SMS. See short message system
Southeast Massachusetts Library System, 75
Squire, Kurt, 62
Steinkuehler, Constance, 62
Sterling, Bruce, 52
Summerfrost, Kristina, 40, 41, 43
Sunday Morning Blog, 28

Teen People Mobile, 18
Teens' comments, 14, 27, 30, 47

Text messaging, definition of, 17
Trillian, 20

Vodcasts, 45, 92, 93
Voice Over Internet Protocol, 15
VOIP. *See* Voice Over Internet
    Protocol

Walker, Jill, 25, 30
Weblog. *See* Blog
Wiki, definition of, 35
Wikipedia, 35, 36, 37, 38, 74,
    90, 92

Yahoo!, 15, 20, 22, 93, 94

About the Author

Linda W. Braun is an educational technology consultant with LEO: Librarians & Educators Online. In her job she works with schools, libraries, and other types of educational institutions to help them figure out the best way to integrate technology into their programs and services. She is also an adjunct faculty member at Simmons College Graduate School of Library and Information Science, where she teaches young adult and technology classes.

Linda provides project management and consulting services to public libraries and schools on a variety of topics and has experience in curriculum and Web site development. Linda has a Masters of Science Degree in Library and Information Science from Simmons College and a Masters of Education with a specialization in Computers in Education from Lesley University.

Linda's publications include *Introducing the Internet to Young Learners: Ready-To-Go Activities and Lesson Plans, The Browsable Classroom: An Introduction to E-Learning for Librarians*, and *Hooking Teens with the Net* (each published by Neal-Schuman). Her books published by the American Library Association are *Teens.Library: Developing Internet Services for Young Adults* and *Technically Involved: Technology-Based Youth Participation Activities for Your Library*. Linda has also authored articles for journals including *netConnect, Library Journal*, and *School Library Journal* and is a columnist for *VOYA*.